BIG
QUESTIONS
IN
CREATIVITY
2016

ICSC PRESS
INTERNATIONAL CENTER *for*
STUDIES *in* CREATIVITY

BUFFALO STATE · The State University of New York

ICSC Press
International Center for Studies in Creativity
Buffalo State, The State University of New York
1300 Elmwood Avenue
Buffalo, NY 14222, USA
icscpress.com

© 2016 by ICSC Press

ISBN: 978-0-9849795-7-8 (print edition)

Library of Congress Control Number: 2013907967

Simultaneously published in multiple formats, both print and electronic. For alternative versions and to discover other titles, visit icscpress.com.

Book Design and Graphics: Kevin D. Opp

BIG
QUESTIONS IN CREATIVITY
2016

EDITED BY
PAUL D. REALI &
CYNTHIA BURNETT

A COLLECTION OF FIRST WORKS, VOLUME 4

ICSC Press
International Center for Studies in Creativity
Buffalo State, The State University of New York
Buffalo, NY, U.S.A.

For the 600 creativity scholars and practitioners who have earned an M.S. in Creativity at the ICSC since its inception, spreading the word and lighting the way for the next 600.

Contents

Introduction

In a small city in upstate New York is a neglected park named for a neglected creative genius, Charles Proteus Steinmetz, a name you almost certainly do not know and have never heard. Steinmetz, a contemporary of Thomas Edison, Nikola Tesla, and Albert Einstein, has mostly disappeared in history, just as his namesake park seems to have been forgotten by the local parks department. Standing just four feet tall, Steinmetz made towering contributions to mathematics and electrical engineering. Among his many quotable statements is this one:

> *There are no foolish questions and no man becomes a fool until he has stopped asking questions.*

Steinmetz did not ask questions in anticipation of having a park bear his name, or of having his name in history books. He asked questions because he had to. The students who arrive each year at the International Center for Studies in Creativity—more than 600 have earned a Master of Science in Creativity here—invariably are the questioning type. And if they are not the questioning types when they arrive, they almost certainly are by the time they leave. Creative thinking *requires* asking questions. Every journey through the Creative Problem Solving process includes such questions as "How to...", "How might...", and "Wouldn't it be great if...." These questions, for those who embrace creativity and creative process, become second nature. They become the *basic questions* that define how we think about our work and our lives.

And then there are the *big questions*.

The study of creativity seems to have another effect on those who study it: the desire to use the lens of the creative thinker to look at the larger world—the big questions that define who we are and what we believe. Each year, ICSC students select a big question they wish to answer, and each year since 2013 ICSC Press publishes the best of these explorations.

The Fourth Edition

Big Questions in Creativity 2016 is the fourth installment featuring first papers in creativity. Each year the editors are impressed by the remarkable breadth of topics and the depth of thinking these emerging scholars exhibit. In each of these papers—each vastly different—we readers get to explore yet another aspect of creativity and how it works in the world.

The essays selected for this anthology are a first foray for their authors in the academic exploration of their creative convictions. Unlike many academic assignments, this one allows the authors to select an area they personally wish to study—a question they feel merits a deep dive. The value in this is apparent in the reading: these writers care deeply about the answers they seek. One of the pleasures of these papers is the way they marry the academic and the personal; several of the papers in each edition include personal stories as a way of illuminating the academic discoveries therein.

While this year's 10 essays address multiple topics, three key themes emerged—organizational creativity, personal creativity, and social capital—and they form the sections of this book.

Organizational Creativity

It is the rare organization that does not say it values creativity and innovation, but how does that play out in the actual workplace?

The collection opens with a look into the future of creativity and innovation and the way in which we understand it. Andrés Mejía-Villa wonders about the next generation of innovation models, finding a rich vein in exploring models of both creativity and innovation and proposing ways for us to model them collectively.

The Organizational Creativity section continues with a sequence of papers that form a kind of conversation about the nature of creativity in business. Celia Pillai begins the conversation by asking how organizations can help to motivate their employees to behave creatively. Diane R. Bessel continues the conversation by digging down into one specific area of creative behavior that concerns organizations, how to build strong problem-solving skills collaboratively, an essential discussion since most organizational creativity is performed in groups. Finally, Karina Loera Barcenas examines small organizations, looking at how an entrepreneur might take his or her own creative mindset and translate that into creative leadership, interweaving a personal story of the consequences and rewards of living with an entrepreneur.

Personal Creativity

Creativity, as is often said in the halls and classrooms of the ICSC, is a life skill. Naturally, then, the personal aspects of creativity provide a deep well of questions for these volumes.

Lina Pugsley explores an area of concern for all of us who are parents and who want our children to share our creative natures, asking what we can actually do to encourage our children's creativity (a topic also explored in editor Burnett's ICSC Press book, *My Sandwich is a Spaceship*). Molly Holinger asks something we have wondered for years, providing an answer at last to the question of why most books on creativity are shelved in the self-help section. The answer, we were glad to read, is located in the connection of creativity to positive psychology, not as a way of discounting the value of creativity as a serious matter of study. To close the section, Rebecca DiLiberto steps confidently into an area some in academia might fear to tread, asking whether one's spiritual intelligence can help cultivate creative potential.

Creativity & Social Capital

The place of creativity in society is far larger than its effects—great as they are—on individuals and organizations. Creativity is a part of our social capital, the substance of what humans bring to this great gathering that humanity is. If we were hermits, lone creatives toiling in our studios, we would have no need to think of social capital—but we are not that. We are in this together.

Mattia Miani starts us off with an investigation into the literature on Eastern and Western approaches to creativity. Does our culture affect our creativity? It doesn't give anything away to tell you that the answer is both yes and no.

Serap Gurak Ozdemir and Virginia L. Bernd then provide bookends, of a sort. Ozdemir looks at the early stages of the creative life, asking whether teachers truly value creativity among their students, and whether we can increase teacher appreciation for creative characteristics through creativity training. Bernd examines later life, asking an equally provocative question: Can we increase the social capital of our aging population by teaching creative thinking? That might be enough of a question to answer, but we were pleased to see the answer go further, into examples of ways we might tap the collective wisdom of our elders.

Conclusion

After four years and 40 published papers, we are thrilled to see that the scholars of the ICSC, as Steinmetz urged, are still asking questions—and even more so, that they are still asking good and important ones. In this volume, like the others, you will find yourself both enlightened on these important questions, and ready to ask some of your own.

Paul D. Reali
Charlotte, NC

Cynthia Burnett
Buffalo, NY

ORGANIZATIONAL
CREATIVITY

What Might Be the Design of a New Generation of Innovation Models?

Andrés Mejía-Villa
University of La Sabana
Bogotá, Colombia

Abstract

These last three decades have seen a growing body of literature on the topic of creativity and innovation. The two constructs have been positioned as independent, complementary, or interchangeable. But, does the same positioning occur with *organizational* models of creativity and innovation? The answer to this overarching question is formulated throughout this paper. A more precise inquiry focuses on the question: What features should be considered for a new generation of innovation models? With that end in mind, this paper discusses the history and definitions of both constructs; describes the contribution that creativity makes to innovation; explains what comprises creativity and innovation models; identifies their approaches, similarities, and differences; and lists their complementary attributes. Finally, this paper concludes by proposing different features for a new generation of innovation models.

What Might Be the Design of a New Generation of Innovation Models?

E verything has changed, is changing, and will continue to change" (Mootee, 2013, p. 1). Expressions like this represent the seemingly-ubiquitous term "VUCA"—that is, a world defined by volatility, uncertainty, complexity, and ambiguity (Lawrence, 2013). These conditions have persisted in challenging the growth, productivity, and competitiveness of the business environment. In response to this vexing challenge, companies have discovered that innovation is the major differentiator in the competitive race (Roberts, 2007). It is no surprise, then, that innovative companies have learned to sustain their competitiveness over long periods of time. According to Bowonder, Dambal, Kumar, and Shirodkar (2010), companies such as Bayer, GE, IBM, P&G, Siemens, and Unilever, as well as newer companies such as Apple, Google, Intel, and Microsoft, have also mastered the mantra of sustained growth and intrinsically have rewritten the rules of the game through a series of innovation strategies (Lawton, Finkelstein, & Harvey, 2007).

However, according to the Oslo Manual,[*] further understanding of the innovation process, and its impact on the economy, is still deficient. For that reason, we need to understand not only if firms are innovative (or not), but we also need to discern how firms innovate and what types of innovations they implement (OECD & Eurostat, 2005). This is important because research suggests that fewer than four percent of the innovation projects undertaken by businesses are proven successful (Kumar, 2012).

Consequently, with the aim to advance the understanding of innovation models and their future developments, this paper seeks to resolve the following research question: *What features should be considered for a new generation of innovation models?* In response, this paper shows a review of the literature to identify the fundamental variables that make up organizational creativity and innovation. Thus, this review considers their separate and sometimes related histories, definitions, approaches, and models to inform features for a new generation of innovation models (see Figure 1). This inquiry not only presents facts about the histories, definitions, approaches, and models of creativity and innovation, but also demonstrates a comparative analysis between the two, which serves as

---

[*] *Oslo Manual: Guidelines for Collecting and Interpreting Innovation Data* (OECD & Eurostat, 2005) is an international source of guidelines for the collection and use of data on innovation activities in industry.

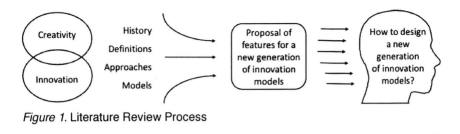

Figure 1. Literature Review Process

a source of knowledge to propose a new generation of innovation models and their characteristics.

Creativity and Innovation: An Ever Closer History

According to Berkhout, Hartmann, Van Der Duin, and Ortt (2006), the economic outlook is changing. They point out that historically, the *classic economy* was based on goods production for local markets through two factors: capital and labor. Subsequently, the increase of production, globalization, competition, the necessity of lower costs, and the demand for specialized products and services served as impetus for a *knowledge economy*, where smarter tools and machines expanded possibilities. Knowledge, therefore, became the third factor of production. For that reason, workforce development evolved as a priority to make companies more efficient. However, Berkhout et al. added, contemporary demands called for another evolution: the *innovation economy*. In this new economy, creativity drove the fourth factor of production. It is important to note that creativity also plays an important role in the knowledge economy, but in the innovation economy, organizational improvement cannot exist without imagination. As Berkhout et al. suggested, one might view the innovation economy as a *creative knowledge economy*.

Xu and Rickards (2007) provided the historical antecedents of the creative knowledge economy by highlighting five stages of evolution: *rational management* (19th-20th century), *incremental innovations* (early 20th century), *humanistic experiments* (mid-20th century), *organizational creativity* (late 20th century), and *creative management* (21st century). The latter of these is considered the study and practice of management, which draws from theories of creative processes and their applications at the individual, group, organizational, and cultural levels. This last stage emerged from the processes embedded in the fourth stage and subsequently offered a focus for revitalizing management theory and practice (Xu & Rickards, 2007). Moreover, one can glimpse the emergence of an integrative process of economics, management, innovation, and creativity.

Creativity and Innovation: Towards a Thematic Conjunction

Predominantly, the literature has defined creativity as the generation of novel and useful ideas, while innovation has been conceived as the production of creative ideas, which is followed by implementation (Amabile, 1996; Shalley & Zhou, 2008; West & Farr, 1990). At the organizational level, creativity is described as "the creation of a valuable, useful new product, service, idea, procedure or process by individuals working together in a complex social system" (Woodman, Sawyer, & Griffin, 1993, p. 293). Meanwhile, the first definition of innovation was coined by Schumpeter (1942) who pointed out that innovation refers to novel outputs; a new good or a new quality of a good; a new method of production; a new market; a new source of supply; or a new organizational structure—all of which can be summarized as "doing things differently." Recently, according to Crossan and Apaydin (2010), innovation was coined as the production or adoption, assimilation, and exploitation of a value-added novelty in economic and social spheres; renewal and enlargement of products, services, and markets; development of new methods of production; and establishment of new management systems. It is both a process and an outcome.* Yet, Anderson, Potočnik, and Zhou (2014) noted the complementary nature of these two constructs. They proffered the following definition:

> Creativity and innovation at work are the process, outcomes, and products of attempts to develop and introduce new and improved ways of doing things. The creativity stage of this process refers to idea generation, and innovation refers to the subsequent stage of implementing ideas toward better procedures, practices, or products. Creativity and innovation can occur at the level of the individual, work team, organization, or at more than one of these levels combined but will invariably result in identifiable benefits at one or more of these levels of analysis. (p. 1298)

The above definition is novel because it incorporates interesting aspects of a systematic view. First, it contains the classic four Ps of creativity (*person, process, product* and *press*) presented by Rhodes (1961) and their innovation counterparts (*people*; repeated creative thinking *processes*; *product* introduction and implementation of strategies; and internal *press* of creation and external

---

*This definition is an abridged version of the current and up-to-date understanding of the concept of innovation as described in the European Commission's (1995) Green Paper on Innovation (pp. 1-2). The original modifier "successful" present in the source was replaced with "value-added" as it would have prevented us from defining innovation ex-ante, before its implementation.

press of the marketplace) proposed by Vehar (2008). Second, this new proposal is in agreement with the *creative change model* described by Puccio, Mance, and Murdock (2010), a systems approach that highlights a set of variables related to organizational creativity (Puccio & Cabra, 2010). Third, this system's view approach is also supported by a multi-dimensional (Crossan & Apaydin, 2010) or multi-level (Drazin, Glynn, & Kazanjian, 1999; Sears & Baba, 2011) view of a creative-innovative process. Finally, the results and benefits of this integrated creative-innovative process are present at all levels (individual, team, organizational, and societal), hence there are partial and final innovation results in each of these levels.

However, Anderson et al.'s (2014) definition does not explicitly consider four relevant topics as seen in the literature review, which is related to a true integration of both concepts: (1) *big purposes,* (2) *open dimension,* (3) *dynamic interaction,* and (4) *leadership and entrepreneurship.* These are important variables to consider in organizational creativity.

Big Purposes

The academic literature positions big purposes in two areas: competitiveness and organizational change. *Competitiveness* is the capacity of people, organizations, and nations to achieve superior outputs and outcomes, and in particular to add value while using the same or lower amounts of inputs (Carayannis & Gonzalez, 2003). From this viewpoint, creativity, innovation, and competitiveness are operationalized at three levels of integration: creativity functions at the individual or micro level, innovation functions at the organizational or meso level, and competitiveness emerges mostly at the national or macro level (Carayannis & Gonzalez, 2003; Tidd, 2001). Similarly, Sears and Baba (2011) pointed out that creativity results from individual innovation, invention from group innovation, adoption from organizational innovation, and organizational and technological change from societal innovation. To be clear, although each level produces its respective outcome, they are integrative and serve the general well-being of the economy. Therefore, it is necessary that this definition have a macro purpose—an all-encompassing view.

The second big purpose is *organizational change.* Creativity and innovation are strategic responses that confront environmental complexity; hence they are considered part of strategic decision making in organizations (Dewett, 2004). Under this perspective, creativity, innovation and organizational change are also integrated. Woodman (2008) presented a *domain model* under which these concepts are integrated in three concentric circles. In the center is organizational creativity, which is surrounded by innovation; and outside this perimeter is organizational change. In this sense, organizational creativity is innovation; all innovation is organizational change; and consequently, all organizational creativity is also change. Similarly, only some organizational changes involve creativity and others innovation. But, innovation always includes creativity. In summary, innovation and organizational creativity support organizational change; and change is vital to support the competitive advantage of organizations (e.g., Damanpour & Schneider, 2006; Damanpour & Wischnevsky, 2006).

Open Dimension

The integrative definition of open dimension provided by Anderson et al. (2014) does not consider the organizations' relationships with other organizations. Their definition of organizational creativity and innovation leaves a space available to recognize the inter- and intra-organizational dimensions of these processes (Camisón & Villar-López, 2014). According to Chesbrough, Vanhaverbeke, and West (2006), *open innovation* is defined as "the use of purposive inflows and outflows of knowledge to accelerate internal innovation, and expand the markets for external use of innovation, respectively" (p. 1). What is more, organizations also need an *open strategy,* which leads them to make strategic sense of innovation communities, ecosystems, networks, and their implications for competitive advantage (Chesbrough & Appleyard, 2007). In sum, a creative-innovative process preconditions an expression of closed and open thinking involving strategy and innovation.

Dynamic Interaction

Although Anderson et al.'s (2014) definition attempts to integrate the creativity and innovation constructs, it does not achieve this objective completely. Cropley and Cropley (2012) explained the classic formula that links both definitions: creativity as the first stage of invention, and after it, innovation as the second stage of exploitation. Thus, invention involves the generation of novel products, processes, systems, and the like, and exploitation involves the implementation of these ideas. According to Rickards (1996), to demarcate creating and implementing is to deny the possibility of organization-wide innovation cultures of "empowered" individuals. For that reason, Rickards asserted that organizations must "stop thinking of the process as divided into the creative bit and the routine bit; start thinking of one unified process in which actions from start to finish are influenced by ideas, and in which ideas are modified by actions and experiences" (p. 22). Rickards also noted that ideas and actions should occur and interact as long as innovation is being pursued. Van de Ven, Polley, Garud, and Venkataraman (2007) proposed viewing innovation as a non-linear dynamic system that consists of a cycle of divergent and convergent activities that may be repeated over time and at different organizational levels. Benner and Tushman (2003) and Burgelman (2002) asserted that creativity and innovation may alternate or occur simultaneously.

Leadership and Entrepreneurship

Anderson et al.'s (2014) integrative definition also does not explicitly include leadership or entrepreneurship. The academic literature has highlighted the relevance of leaders for group and organizational creativity (e.g., Gumusluoglu & Ilsev, 2009; Rickards & Moger, 2006; Sternberg, 2003). According to Puccio, Mance, and Murdock (2011), leadership is the lubricant that allows the other elements to effectively interact or, in some cases, not. Effective leadership begins by establishing a creative atmosphere that supports people as they engage in creative thinking processes. For that reason, Puccio et al. positioned leadership as a fundamental part of their *creative change model*. To be clear, the authors defined *creative leadership* as:

> [T]he ability to deliberately engage one's imagination to define and guide a group toward a novel goal—a direction that is new for the group. As a consequence of bringing about this creative change, creative leaders have a profoundly positive influence on their context and the individuals in that situation. (Puccio et al., 2011, p. 28)

In parallel, Berkhout et al. (2006) explained that entrepreneurship plays a central role: "Without entrepreneurship there is no innovation" (p. 397). Drucker (1998) also highlighted the importance of this topic when he pointed out that "innovation is the specific function of entrepreneurship.... It is the means by which the entrepreneur either creates new wealth-producing resources or endows existing resources with enhanced potential for creating wealth" (p. 3).

Summarizing, the proximity of both constructs requires a cohesive definition that shows creativity and innovation as integrated, interactive, iterative, closed and open processes, guided and motivated by a creative leadership, with different inter- and intra-organizational levels, which work together for the purpose of creating and capturing value.

Functional and Sense Making Paradigms: Two Approaches to Understand Creativity and Innovation

Drazin, Kazanjian, and Glynn (2008) pointed out that social and organizational theories are constructed based upon implicit and explicit assumptions about human behavior. Therefore Wagner and Berger (1985) argued that these assumptions govern what questions we ask, the models we create, and the approach we use to test our models. In that sense, Drazin et al. (2008) presented two schools of thought to explain the organizational processes of creativity and innovation. The first is the *structural-functional paradigm*, which has dominated the sociological and management literature. In this approach, the processes of creativity or innovation are presumed to be in a functional or contributory relationship with a large social system in which it is embedded (Drazin et al., 2008). Thus, this paradigm has a deterministic orientation; behavior is orderly, rational, and constrained by externalities. Outcomes dominate as criteria of action, and change occurs primarily through a division of labor into creative and productive roles that are assumed to integrate harmoniously (Parsons, 1951). In this perspective, creativity and innovation are regarded as important *outcomes* to the social system, and independent variables are considered as factors to be manipulated to improve these outcomes.

In contrast, the second school of thought is *sense making*. This perspective has made significant research progress (Burrell & Morgan, 1979); albeit, the functionalist perspective dominates organizational research (Gioia & Pitre, 1990). Accordingly, Drazin et al. (2008) stressed an understanding of the process through which individuals and organizations develop systems of meaning and how these systems of meaning lead to the emergence of a stream of organizational behavior over time. Thus, the sense making perspective is useful to describe creative and innovative processes. Consequently, under this view creativity and innovation are considered processes rather than outcomes. For that reason, a multilevel organizational analysis under this perspective comprises the same levels as the functionalist approach but focuses on the process of each one rather than their results. Thus, according to Weick (1995), the individual level refers to an *intra-subjective process*—hence the cognitive processes; group level is denominated by an *intersubjective level* because there exist shared frames of references by several people; and the organizational level is the *collective level* that represents the unfolding of change across intersubjective levels.

That said, if these perspectives determine the points of view to understand creativity and innovation, as well as their organizational models, then which are the models under both perspectives?

Innovation and Creativity Models

In this section, different types of innovation and creativity models are presented. In that sense, models such as Stage-Gate (Cooper, 2008), Design-driven Innovation (Verganti, 2009), Design Thinking (Brown, 2008), Theory of Inventive Problem Solving-TRIZ (Mann, 2001), and others, are not considered here because their approaches are related with particular applications, specific aspects, or steps about innovation management rather than general kind of creativity and/or innovation models. Even these could be classified as specific cases or expressions of a general typology of models of creativity and innovation, which are presented below.

Organizational Innovation Models

In the innovation literature, innovation models are subdivided into generations (Berkhout et al., 2006), with the aim of explaining how all models came together to generate commercially viable technologies (Marinova & Phillimore, 2003). Thus, several authors have presented different classifications of these generations. Generally, they present a chronological classification of technological innovation models. In this sense, Rothwell (1994) pointed to the existence of four generations (*Technology Push, Market Pull, Couplin Model,* and *Integrated Innovation*), and proposed a fifth (*Systems Integration and Networking models*), which was formalized and explained by Hobday (2005).

Marinova and Phillimore (2003) described six generations, the largest number found in these studies. Their sequence: *Black Box Model* (Hobday, 2005; Rothwell, 1994); *Linear* models (Technology Push and Market Pull); *Interactive* and *Systems* models (which parallel Systems Integration and Networking models from Hobday, 2005); *Evolutionary Model;* and *Innovative Milieu.* Cropley and Cropley (2012) developed a complete synthesis of these six models based on their foci, strengths, and weakness.

With the same chronological logic, Berkhout et al. (2006) recognized the first three generation models from Rothwell (1994), then proposed a fourth generation: the *Cyclic Innovation Model.* This is characterized by open innovation partnerships, interaction between science and business, hard knowledge of emerging technologies complemented by soft knowledge of emerging markets, new organizational concepts such as skills for managing networks with specialized suppliers and early users, and a central role of entrepreneurship.

From another point of view, Chesbrough (2003) presented two types of models: *Closed* and *Open Innovation* (see also Herzog, 2011). He pointed out that the old model of *Closed Innovation* adhered to the following philosophy: successful innovation requires control. In other words, companies must generate their own ideas which they will then develop, manufacture, market, distribute and service themselves. In contrast, he presented the new model of *Open Innovation,* in which the boundary between a firm and its surrounding environment is more porous, enabling innovation to move easily between the two (Chesbrough, 2003). This might include deploying outside pathways to the market, commercializing internal ideas through channels outside of their current businesses, and using ideas that originate outside the firm's own labs and are brought inside for commercialization.

Organizational Creativity Models

Drazin et al. (2008) pointed out that in the early 1980s and into the 1990s, creativity researchers extended their models beyond the study of individuals (Ford, 1996; Woodman et al., 1993) to include the effects of group or team-level variables (Amabile, 1988). Thus, the *Componential Model of Creativity and Innovation in Organizations* developed by Amabile (1988) is based on individual creativity but also describes the impact of that creativity on organizational innovation. According to Borghini (2005), the implicit idea behind Amabile's model is that creative behavior can be developed only on the individual level and that cognitive and creative skills, and especially motivation, are more important than norms, routines (March, 1991; Nelson & Winter, 1982), and shared behavior.

Another model is *Creative Problem Solving (CPS)*, an evolving group of models based on the work Osborn and extended by Parnes and others, comprising at least ten developments and spin-offs (Puccio, Murdock, & Mance, 2005). CPS can be thought of as a cognitive process with applications for individuals and groups. The original CPS model presented by Osborn (1953) included seven steps: (1) orientation, (2) preparation, (3) analysis, (4) hypothesis, (5) incubation, (6) synthesis, and (7) verification. One of the most recent versions was developed by Puccio, Mance, and Murdock (2011), and is called *CPS: The Thinking Skills Model*. It has three major stages (clarification, transformation, and implementation) and seven discrete steps (from Exploring Challenges to Formulating a Plan). The model also includes seven thinking skills (diagnostic, visionary, strategic, ideational, evaluative, contextual, and tactical) and seven affective skills (curiosity, dreaming, sensing gaps, playfulness, avoiding premature closure, sensitivity to environment, and tolerance for risks) associated with the model's seven steps.

In contrast to the above models that are based on individual and group levels, in a very few cases organizational-level variables have been incorporated into models of creativity (Drazin et al., 2008). Factors such as organizational policies, structures, and climate (Burkhardt & Brass, 1990; Tushman & Nelson, 1990), as well as organization-wide training of individuals (Basadur, Graen, & Scandura, 1986; Wheatley, Anthony, & Maddox, 1991) have been linked to creative output. The most comprehensive theoretical model that includes creativity at the organizational level is offered by Woodman et al. (1993), who linked culture, resources, technology, strategy, and rewards to creativity. This process is called the *Interactionist Model of Creativity*, and it considers creativity at the organizational level like a sum of efforts from the group level, and group-level creativity like a sum of individual creativity.

Previous models are based on the functionalist paradigm. In contrast, a sensemaking approach (Weick, 1995) is presented by Borghini (2005) who showed a dynamic creative process based on processes of cultural integration, the creation of new knowledge, and the codification of knowledge through integration and sharing. In this process, the solution of problems generates new knowledge, which then develops new competencies, which in turn are shared with different cultural groups within the organization. Consequently, the integration among the different cultures of the dominions in question represent the necessary condition for generating the stock of new knowledge and essential competencies to problem solving (Nonaka, 1991). However, this process represents at the same time the generation of *core rigidities* as a result of codifying knowledge in the organization. These become *organizational rigidities* that mean the inability to abandon rules and consolidated knowledge which have proved to be effective in the past. In a negative way, this affects the creative process. For that reason, the organization requires another kind of process: the destruction of previously-acquired competencies and the manifestation of changes in the cultures of the business sub-systems (Borghini, 2005).

Previously, we studied several different models of creativity and innovation. In the next section, we will develop a comparative analysis of creativity and innovation processes with the aim of finding common and divergent aspects between the two processes.

An Analysis of Organizational Innovation and Creativity Models

Innovation models emerged from the world of economics, which consider innovation as an endogenous change (an internal effort from company to change). Schumpeter (1942), an economist, pointed out that the innovation process was a fundamental driver of economic development, as reflected through his concept of *creative destruction*. To be precise, Schumpeter posited that innovation represents the "process of industrial mutation that incessantly revolutionizes the economic structure from within, incessantly destroying the old one, incessantly creating a new one" (p. 81). Today, after much progress, the economics of innovation seem to concentrate more and more on the effort to elaborate a theory of economic creativity that highlights organizational development and decision (Antonelli, 2014). On the other hand, the study of organizational creative models generally has arisen from psychology because the main studies have been at the individual level. Additionally, other approaches have emerged in social disciplines (Mayer, 1999; Sternberg & Lubart, 1999) such as psychometric, cognitive, social and contextual (including cultural and evolutionary), and experimental. These different foundations of creativity and innovation models explain the gap between both, which is the same that exists between microeconomics and psychology. Therefore, to address the gap, a multilevel relationship could exist in which psychology could serve to underpin the economic dynamic of organizational innovation.

A second point in this comparative analysis is the contrast that exists between the innovation model generations and their additive characters (that is, new models add new concepts to old models, therefore, the old and new knowledge is integrated into one body), and the organizational creativity models which are not integrative (old and new models are not integrated with each other). For example, using Marinova and Phillimore's (2003) generations of innovation models, the Linear Model (as an innovation model) is included in the practices of the next Couplin Model generation; the Integrated Model forms part of the Systems Integration and Networking models; and they too form part of the Innovative Milieu models. Meanwhile, the Cyclic Innovation Model (Berkhout et al., 2006) includes the evolutionary and systemic approach taken from previous models. Therefore, this shows an evolutionary knowledge-building process that makes salient an innovation model phenomenon. In contrast, the different models of creativity are not necessarily interrelated and therefore they are not complementary; rather, they are equivalent. For that reason, an organization could use only the Interactionist Model by Woodman et al. (1993), the Componential Model by Amabile (1988), or the model by Borghini (2005), but an organization could not use an integrated creative model as a result of the union of these models.

A third point is that a model does not exist that fully integrates organizational creativity and innovation models. The Componential Model (Amabile, 1988) links both processes but essentially this is a proposal of individual creativity, which is related to the linear innovation process. Here, creativity is considered the first part of the innovation process but there is not a mix between both models. The Cyclic Innovation Model (Berkhout et al., 2006) includes creativity and it discusses its relevance, but creativity practices are diluted at the midpoint of the innovation process.

Generally, the models of creativity and innovation have been designed from the structural-functional paradigm (according to explanation above). For that reason, they are systems with clearly-identified dependent and independent variables. Models like the linear ones (Technology Pull and Market Pull), Couplin, Integrated, Componential, Interactionist, CPS, Evolutionary, Innovative Milieu, and Cyclic Innovation Model (Amabile, 1988; Marinova & Phillimore, 2003; Puccio et al., 2011; Rothwell, 1994) are based on factors that nurture creativity and innovation in one or various levels. The aim, therefore, is to improve these factors to increase creativity and innovation, which under these conditions are considered outcomes. On the other hand, only the Borghini (2005) creativity model presented a process based on a sense-making approach that features an understanding of the process rather than outcomes (see explanation above).

A final point arises from observations made of the development of both creativity and innovation models that affirm a forward trajectory towards more complex, flexible, and open models, generations more akin to a global business context (see e.g., Gassmann, Enkel, & Chesbrough, 2010; Huizingh, 2011; Niosi, 1999; Tidd, Bessant, & Pavitt, 2005). This occurs because organizations need to respond to the escalating pace and volume of change and the complexity and more intense competition that it brings (Isaksen & Tidd, 2006). The innovation side shows the increase of complexity, flexibility, and openness through the advance between the old Linear Models and the new Systematics, Evolutionary, Cyclic, and Milieu models (Marinova & Phillimore, 2003). On the creativity side, the process has developed, too. It has evolved from Componential (Amabile, 1988) and Interactionist (Woodman et al., 1993) models to CPS: The Thinking Skill Model (Puccio et al., 2011) and Borghini's (2005) creativity model. Both models characterize an exploration of the complexity of cognitive processes, organizational culture and its knowledge management.

Additionally, according to Tidd (2006), the innovation models (and it is possible to include creativity models here, too) are characterized by a partial understanding of the innovation process; as a consequence, the models have been conceived like linear processes and as such miss the potential of incremental innovation, consider innovation as a single isolated change rather than as part of a wider system, and see innovation as product or process without recognizing the interrelationship between the two. In the same way, Tidd et al. (2005) presented the following problems of this partial view of innovation: considering R&D as the main capability; thinking that innovation is only for specialist or key individuals; understanding only the customer needs or only the technology advances; thinking this topic targets only large and single firms; developing only radical innovation; managing innovation only through strategic projects; and considering only a closed or open development of innovation.

Recommendations

Throughout this paper, the contrast between creativity and innovation was shown, related to their histories, definitions, approaches, and models, so that different features can be considered for developing a new generation of innovation models. With this aim in mind, this study uses the *Multi-dimensional Framework of Organizational Innovation* proposed by Crossan and Apaydin (2010) as a basis for its proposal because it offers a clear way to understand different sources and results of innovation. Thus, this framework has ten dimensions to depict innovation as a process and outcome (see Table 1). Additionally, this study has added three dimensions as categories that have arisen from the previous analysis developed in this research; these are: *foundation, sequence* and *purpose*. Table

1 synthesizes the proposal's conclusions along three parts: (1) 13 dimensions as categories of characteristics; (2) current features found as a result of the previous analysis; and, (3) the proposal of features that enhance, complement, and adapt current features to better reflect environmental complexity and dynamism, which will be used in the future for designing a new generation of innovation models. The core of this proposal is the integration and interaction of creativity and innovation processes, as they are complementary and synergetic. This is part of their nature. Therefore, they are not sequential actions (Burgelman, 2002; Rickards, 1996) as the analysis showed above. To distinguish this interaction, this article proposes features for designing a new generation of innovation models as shown on the second column in Table 1 as "Creativity+Innovation (C+I)." Column one lists the current features of creative and innovation models.

As seen in Table 1, the first dimension is *foundation*. Thus, although creativity and innovation have different sources, it is necessary to develop a dialogue in which the economics of innovation considers psychology as its core. In this integration both require a consideration for the functional paradigm and sense making as two perspectives from which is possible to understand C+I (Borghini, 2005; Drazin et al., 2008; Weick, 1995).

The second dimension is *sequence*. Here the linear or cyclic shape of the process is emphasized. The conclusion is that new innovation models could be evolutionary, cyclic, and iterative as responses to a complex and dynamic business environment, which requires constant adaptation (Berkhout et al. 2006; Kumar, 2012; Nelson & Winter, 1982). Likewise, future models should depict an interaction between creativity and innovation along this process (Burgelman, 2002; Rickards, 1996) and through all *levels* of the organization, because C+I is a system in which each one participates and affects the others' levels.

Direction is the dimension that covers the flow of ideas and motivation of this process. Here, participation and commitment come from all people (bottom-up); new processes fuse creative leadership and entrepreneurship, which encourages people, accompanies the C+I process, and obtains effective results (Berkhout et al., 2006; Drucker, 1998; Puccio et al., 2011). With this cyclic, iterative, and interactive process, both customers and technology are *drivers* of a C+I process (Tidd, 2006; Tidd et al., 2005), as the success is achieved when there is fit between value proposition (technology side) and customer segment (Osterwalder, Pigneur, Bernarda, & Smith, 2014). New innovation models, therefore, require the invention and adoption as a *source* to a C+I process. This suggests that there are internal and external sources. Therefore, organizations need to develop a mix between closed and open innovation (Chesbrough & Appleyard, 2007; Chesbrough et al., 2006).

In the same sense, the dimension denominated as *locus* explains the context of the C+I process. The proposal, therefore, suggests developing networks as a response to new conditions under which cooperation, integration, and parallel development are considered effective innovation (Hobday, 2005; Rothwell, 1994;). Likewise, these network are propitious spaces for all kind of organizations (Tidd, 2006; Tidd et al., 2005) which develop a mix of closed and open innovations (Gupta, Smith, & Shalley, 2006).

The *nature* of knowledge for new models suggests that C+I will be a process of learning and unlearning by which people and teams transform and adjust tacit knowledge to explicit knowledge that permits the sharing of mental models to develop the C+I process (Borghini, 2005). The next dimension is the *form* of innovation, which for a next generation would comprise a mix of all types of innovation outcomes as consequence of an integrative, systemic, and complex C+I process that generates outcomes at each level. In the same way, the *purpose* dimension will be defined by the big purpose of C+I process: organizational change at the organizational level (Woodman, 2008), and competitiveness at organizational and macro levels (Carayannis & Gonzalez, 2003).

The *referent* dimension explains that new models will need to consider incremental changes to improve the organization, innovations that reach and discover new markets, and innovations that generate competitiveness within the industry. The *magnitude* dimension proposes a mix of incremental and radical innovations (Tidd, 2006; Tidd et al., 2005). Finally, the *type* dimension represents the difference between creativity and innovation processes based on technical or administrative developments. Today, organizations require many types of C+I based on magnitude, form, level, and purpose dimensions.

In summary, the increase of complexity and dynamism of the business context demands that companies and institutions integrate creativity and innovation through an organizational process characterized by flexibility, continuous learning, open-closed and systemic views, thinking and affective skills, valuation of incremental and radical results, multi-level interaction, and effective leadership and entrepreneurship.

Table 1. *A proposal of features to design a new generation of innovation models*

Dimensions of Innovation	From current features of creativity and innovation (C+I) models…	…to features for designing a new generation of creativity and innovation (C+I) models
Foundation: knowledge foundations	Innovation is based on economics of innovation (Antonelli, 2014; Nelson & Winter, 1982; Schumpeter, 1942). Creativity is based on psychology and social disciplines (Mayer, 1999; Sternberg & Lubart, 1999).	Dialogue between economics and psychology underpin a new generation of C+I models.
	Creativity and innovation approaches are developed from structural-functional paradigm (Drazin et al., 2008).	C+I approach is developed from a structural-functional paradigm and sensemaking perspective (Borghini, 2005; Drazin et al., 2008; Weick, 1995).
Sequence: lineal or cyclic	Linear view of the creativity and innovation processes (Tidd, 2006; Tidd et al., 2005).	Evolutionary, cyclic and iterative view of the C+I process (Berkhout et al., 2006; Kumar, 2012; Nelson & Winter, 1982; Nickles, 2003).
Sequence: stepwise or continuous	Creativity as first stage of ideation, and innovation as second stage of implementation (Amabile, 1988; Bledow, Frese, Anderson, Erez, & Farr, 2009; Cropley & Cropley, 2012; Luecke & Katz, 2003; Roberts, 1988).	Creativity and innovation interact throughout the whole process and through all levels (Burgelman, 2002; Rickards, 1996; Van de Ven et al., 2007).
Level: individual, group, organization or macro	Creativity and innovation is a topic dedicated to specialists and key people (Tidd, 2006; Tidd et al., 2005).	C+I concerns all people from the firm and its partners outside the company.
	Creativity and innovation developed for some levels (Amabile, 1988; Puccio et al., 2005; Woodman et al., 1993).	C+I are developed according to an integrative view. It requires a systemic perspective (Puccio et al., 2007; Sears & Baba, 2011).

(Table continues next page)

Table 1. *A proposal of features to design a new generation of innovation models (continued)*

Dimensions of Innovation (cont.)	From current features of creativity and innovation (C+I) models... (cont.)	...to features for designing a new generation of creativity and innovation (C+I) models (cont.)
Direction: top-down or bottom-up	Creativity and innovation without the core role of leadership and entrepreneurship.	Fusion between creative leadership and entrepreneurship as a core element of the C+I process (Berkhout et al., 2006; Drucker, 1998; Puccio et al., 2011).
Driver: resources or market opportunity	Customers or technology are drivers of creativity and innovation (Tidd, 2006; Tidd et al., 2005).	C+I considered both customers and technology drivers of its process (Tidd, 2006; Tidd et al., 2005); success is reached when there is a fit between value proposition and customer segment (Osterwalder et al., 2014).
Source: invention or adoption	Innovation is a process centered at closed invention.	This is an open and closed (ambidextrous) process that uses invention and adoption as sources of the process (Chesbrough et al., 2006; Chesbrough & Appleyard, 2007).
Locus: firm or network	Creativity and innovation are alone firm issues (Tidd, 2006; Tidd et al., 2005).	C+I is a network issue (Hobday, 2005; Rothwell, 1994).
	These topics are only for big enterprises (Tidd, 2006; Tidd et al., 2005).	This is for all kinds of firms (Tidd, 2006; Tidd et al., 2005).
	Mainly a closed innovation process and sometimes open (Tidd, 2006; Tidd et al., 2005).	A mix of closed and open innovation that develops ambidexterity capabilities (Gupta et al., 2006)
Nature: Tacit or explicit	Creativity and innovation processes uses explicit knowledge.	It is a process of learning and unlearning by which people and teams transform and adjust tacit knowledge; explicit knowledge informs shared mental models to further develop the C+I process (Borghini, 2005).
		(Table continues next page)

Table 1. A proposal of features to design a new generation of innovation models (continued)

Dimensions of Innovation (cont.)	From current features of creativity and innovation (C+I) models... (cont.)	...to features for designing a new generation of creativity and innovation (C+I) models (cont.)
Form: product, service, process or business model	This is about product/service or process as outcomes (Tidd, 2006; Tidd et al., 2005).	This is an integrative, systemic and complex process that mixes all ways of innovation outcomes to reach the purposes (Keeley, Walters, Pikkel, & Quinn, 2013).
Purpose: immediate or long term outcomes	Products, services, process, structures, practices, etc, as outcomes.	Competitiveness and organizational change as big purposes of C+I process (Carayannis & Gonzalez, 2003; Woodman, 2008).
Referent: firm, market or industry	The company develops creativity and innovation processes to further its position in the market and to maintain its competitiveness.	The C+I process of a company is a way to change itself. Also, it permits it to reach and discover new markets and to be competitive in its cluster in a specific moment.
Magnitude: incremental or radical	This is a topic of radical innovation (Tidd, 2006; Tidd et al., 2005).	C+I is a process that considers incremental and radical innovations (Tidd, 2006; Tidd et al., 2005).
Type: administrative or technical	Creativity and innovation are developed through strategic projects, mostly at a technological level (Tidd, 2006; Tidd et al., 2005).	C+I is a process developed through projects or incremental effective changes involving many topics. It is developed daily, and along the firm and its industry or cluster.

Note: C+I = The combination, interaction and integration of creativity and innovation processes.
Source: Author's analysis and synthesis, and listed authors as cited.

Acknowledgments

The author appreciates the support received from Associate Professor John Cabra and International Center for Studies in Creativity at SUNY Buffalo State during his visit to the college. Likewise, he appreciates the feedback provided by the Innovation Decisions in the Business Environment Research Group at the School of Economics from University of Navarra (Spain). His visit to Buffalo State and his doctoral studies have been possible by the financial support of the University of La Sabana (Colombia).

References

Amabile, T. M. (1988). A model of creativity and innovation in organizations. In B. M. Staw & L. L. Cummings (Eds.), *Research in organizational behavior* (pp. 123-167). Greenwich, CT: JAI Press.

Amabile, T. M. (1996). *Creativity in context.* Boulder, CO: Westview.

Anderson, N., Potočnik, K., & Zhou, J. (2014). Innovation and creativity in organizations: A state-of-the-science review, prospective commentary, and guiding framework. *Journal of Management, 40*(5), 1297-1333.

Antonelli, C. (2014). *The economics of innovation, new technologies and structural change.* New York, NY: Routledge.

Basadur, M., Graen, G. B., & Scandura, T. A. (1986). Teaching effects on attitudes toward divergent thinking among manufacturing engineers. *Journal of Applied Psychology, 71,* 612-617.

Benner, M. J., & Tushman, M. (2003). Exploitation, exploration, and process management: The productivity dilemma revisited. *Academy of Management Review, 27,* 238-256.

Berkhout, A. J., Hartmann, D., Van Der Duin, P., & Ortt, R. (2006). Innovating the innovation process. *International Journal of Technology Management, 34*(3-4), 390-404.

Bledow, R., Frese, M., Anderson, N., Erez, M., & Farr, J. (2009). A dialectic perspective on innovation: Conflicting demands, multiple pathways, and ambidexterity. *Industrial and Organizational Psychology, 2*(3), 305-337.

Borghini, S., (2005). Organizational creativity: Breaking equilibrium and order to innovate. *Journal of Knowledge Management, 9*(4), 19-33.

Bowonder, B., Dambal, A., Kumar, S., & Shirodkar, A. (2010). Innovation strategies for creating competitive advantage. *Research-Technology Management, 53*(3), 19-32.

Brown, T. (2008). Design thinking. *Harvard Business Review, 86*(6), 84-93.

Burgelman, R. A. (2002). Strategy as vector and the inertia of co-evolutionary lock-in. *Administrative Science Quarterly, 47*, 325-357.

Burkhardt, M. E., & Brass, D. J. (1990). Changing patterns or patterns of change: The effects of change in technology on social network structure and power. *Administrative Science Quarterly, 35*, 1-8.

Burrell, G., & Morgan, G. (1979). *Sociological paradigms and organizational analysis.* London, UK: Heinemann.

Camisón, C., & Villar-López, A. (2014). Organizational innovation as an enabler of technological innovation capabilities and firm performance. *Journal of Business Research, 67*(1), 2891-2902.

Carayannis, E. G., & Gonzalez, E., (2003). Creativity and innovation = competitiveness? When, how and why. In L. V. Shavinina (Ed.), *The international handbook on innovation* (pp. 587-606). Oxford, UK: Elsevier Press.

Chesbrough, H. W. (2003). The era of open innovation. *MIT Sloan Management Review, 44*(3), 35-41.

Chesbrough, H. W., & Appleyard, M. M. (2007). Open innovation and strategy. *California Management Review, 50*(1), 57-76.

Chesbrough, H. W., Vanhaverbeke, W., & West, J. (2006). *Open innovation: Researching a new paradigm.* Oxford, UK: Oxford University Press.

Cooper, R. G. (2008). Perspective: The Stage-Gate idea-to-launch process— Update, what's new and nexgen systems. *Journal of Product Innovation Management, 25*(3), 213-232.

Cropley, D., & Cropley, A. (2012). A psychological taxonomy of organizational innovation: Resolving the paradoxes. *Creativity Research Journal, 24*(1), 29-40.

Crossan, M. M., & Apaydin, M. (2010). A multi-dimensional framework of organizational innovation: A systematic review of the literature. *Journal of Management Studies, 47*, 1154-1192.

Damanpour, F., & Schneider, M. (2006). Phases of the adoption of innovation in organizations: Effects of environment, organization, and top managers. *British Journal of Management, 17*, 215-236.

Damanpour, F., & Wischnevsky, J. D. (2006). Research on organizational innovation: Distinguishing innovation-generating from innovation-adopting organizations. *Journal of Engineering and Technology Management, 23,* 269-291.

Dewett, T. (2004). Creativity and strategic management: Individual and group considerations concerning decision alternatives in the top management teams. *Journal of Managerial Psychology, 19*(2), 156-169.

Drazin, R., Glynn, M.A., & Kazanjian, R. K. (1999), Multilevel theorizing about creativity in organizations: A sense-making perspective. *Academy of Management Review, 24*(2), 286-307.

Drazin, R., Kazanjian, R., & Glynn, M. (2008). Creativity and sensemaking among professionals. In J. Zhou & C. E. Shalley (Eds.), *Handbook of organizational creativity* (pp. 263-282). New York, NY: Lawrence Erlbaum Associates.

Drucker, P. F. (1998). The discipline of innovation. *Harvard Business Review, 76*(6), 149-157.

European Commission (1995, December). *Green paper on innovation.* Retrieved from http://cordis.europa.eu/publication/rcn/361_en.html

Ford, C. M. (1996). A theory of individual creativity in multiple social domains. *Academy of Management Review, 21,* 1112-1134.

Gassmann, O., Enkel, E., & Chesbrough, H. (2010). The future of open innovation. *R&D Management, 40*(3), 213-221.

Gioia, D. A., & Pitre, E. (1990). Multiparadigm perspectives on theory building. *Academy of Management Review, 4,* 584-602.

Gumusluoglu, L., & Ilsev, A. (2009). Transformational leadership, creativity, and organizational innovation. *Journal of Business Research, 62*(4), 461-473.

Gupta, A. K., Smith, K. G., & Shalley, C. E. (2006). The interplay between exploration and exploitation. *Academy of Management Journal, 49,* 693-706.

Herzog, P. (2011). *Open and closed innovation: Different cultures for different strategies* (2nd ed.). Wiesbaden, Germany: Springer Science & Business Media.

Hobday, M. (2005). Firm-level innovation models: Perspectives on research in developed and developing countries. *Technology Analysis & Strategic Management, 17*(2), 121-146.

Huizingh, E. K. (2011). Open innovation: State of the art and future perspectives. *Technovation, 31*(1), 2-9.

Isaksen, S., & Tidd, J. (2006). *Meeting the innovation challenge.* West Sussex, UK: John Wiley & Sons.

Keeley, L., Walters, H., Pikkel, R., & Quinn, B. (2013). *Ten types of innovation: The discipline of building breakthroughs.* Hoboken, NJ: John Wiley & Sons.

Kumar, V. (2012). *101 design methods: A structured approach for driving innovation in your organization.* Hoboken, NJ: John Wiley & Sons.

Lawrence, K. (2013). *Developing leaders in a VUCA environment.* [Unpublished manuscript.]

Lawton, T., Finkelstein, S., & Harvey, C. (2007). Taking by storm: A breakthrough strategy. *Journal of Business Strategy, 28*(2), 22-29.

Luecke, R., & Katz, R. (2003). *Managing creativity and innovation.* Boston, MA: Harvard Business School Press.

Mann, D. (2001). An introduction to TRIZ: The theory of inventive problem solving. *Creativity and Innovation Management, 10*(2), 123-125.

March, J. G. (1991). Exploration and exploitation in organizational learning. *Organization Science, 2*(1), 71-87.

Marinova, D., & Phillimore, J. (2003). Models of innovation. In L. V. Shavinina (Ed.), *The international handbook on innovation* (pp. 44-53). London, UK: Pergamon.

Mayer, R. E. (1999). Fifty years of creativity research. In R. J. Sternberg (Ed.), *Handbook of creativity* (pp. 449-460). Cambridge, UK: Cambridge University Press.

Mootee, I. (2013). *Design thinking for strategic innovation: What they can't teach you at business or design school.* Hoboken, NJ: John Wiley & Sons.

Nelson, R. R., & Winter, S. (1982). *An evolutionary theory of economic change.* Cambridge, MA: Harvard University Press.

Nickles, T. (2003). Evolutionary models of innovation and the meno problem. In L. V. Shavinina (Ed.), *The international handbook on innovation* (pp. 54-78). London, UK: Pergamon.

Niosi, J. (1999). Fourth-generation R&D: From linear models to flexible innovation. *Journal of Business Research, 45,* 111-117.

Nonaka, I. (1991). The knowledge-creating company. *Harvard Business Review, 69*(6), 96-104.

OECD and Eurostat (2005). *Oslo Manual: Guidelines for collecting and interpreting innovation data* (3rd ed.). Paris, France: OECD Publishing.

Osborn, A. F. (1953). *Applied imagination: Principles and procedures of creative thinking.* New York, NY: Charles Scribner's Sons.

Osterwalder, A., Pigneur, Y., Bernarda, G., & Smith, A. (2014). *Value proposition design: How to create products and services customers want.* Hoboken, NJ: John Wiley & Sons.

Parsons, T. (1951). *The social system.* Glencoe, IL: Free Press.

Puccio, G. J., & Cabra, J. F. (2010). Organizational creativity: A systems approach. In J. C. Kaufman & R. J. Sternberg (Eds.), *The Cambridge handbook of creativity* (pp. 145-173). Cambridge, UK: Cambridge University Press.

Puccio, G. J., Mance, M., & Murdock, M. C. (2011). *Creative leadership: Skills that drive change* (2nd ed.). Thousand Oaks, CA: SAGE Publications.

Puccio, G. J., Murdock, M. C., & Mance, M. (2005). Current developments in creative problem solving for organizations: A Focus on thinking skills and styles. *The Korean Journal of Thinking & Problem Solving, 15*(2), 43-76.

Rhodes, M. (1961). An analysis of creativity. *Phi Delta Kappan, 4*, 305-310.

Rickards, T. (1996). The management of innovation: Recasting the role of creativity. *European Journal of Work and Organizational Psychology, 5*(1), 13-27.

Rickards, T., & Moger, S. (2006). Creative leaders: A decade of contributions from Creativity and Innovation Management Journal. *Creativity and Innovation Management, 15*(1), 4-18.

Roberts, E. B. (2007). Managing invention and innovation. *Research Technology Management, 49*(1), 35-54.

Roberts, E. D. (1988). What we have learned managing invention and innovation. *Research Technology Management, 1*, 11-29.

Rothwell, R. (1994). Towards the fifth-generation innovation process. *International Marketing Review, 11*(1), 7-31.

Schumpeter, J. A. (1942). *Capitalism, socialism, and democracy.* New York, NY: Harper & Brothers.

Sears, G. J., & Baba, V. V. (2011). Toward a multistage, multilevel theory of innovation. *Canadian Journal of Administrative Sciences / Revue Canadienne des Sciences de l'Administration, 28*(4), 357-372.

Shalley, C. E., & Zhou, J. (2008). Organizational creativity research: A historical overview. In J. Zhou & C. E. Shalley (Eds.), *Handbook of organizational creativity* (pp. 3-31). Hillsdale, NJ: Lawrence Erlbaum Associates.

Sternberg, R. J. (2003). WICS: A model of leadership in organizations. *Academy of Management Learning & Education*, 2(4), 386-401.

Sternberg, R. J., & Lubart, T. I. (1999). The concept of creativity: Prospects and paradigms. In R. J. Sternberg (Ed.), *Handbook of creativity* (pp. 3-15). Cambridge, UK: Cambridge University Press.

Tidd, J. (2001). Innovation management in context: Environment, organization and performance. *International Journal of Managerial Reviews*, 3(3), 169-183.

Tidd, J. (2006). *A review of innovation models.* Imperial College London. Retrieved from http://ict.udlap.mx/projects/cudi/sipi/files/Innovation%20 models%20Imperial%20College%20London.pdf

Tidd, J., Bessant, J., & Pavitt, K. (2005). *Managing innovation: Integrating technological, market and organizational change.* New York, NY: Wiley.

Tushman, M. L., & Nelson, R. R. (1990). Introduction: Technology, organizations, and innovation. *Administrative Science Quarterly, 35,* 1-8

Van de Ven, A., Polley, D., Garud, S., & Venkataraman, S. (2007). *The innovation journey.* New York, NY: Oxford University Press.

Vehar, J. (2008, May). Creativity and innovation: A call for rigor in language. In G. J. Puccio et al. (Eds.), *Proceedings from An International Conference on Creativity and Innovation Management—The Second Community Meeting,* Vol. 2 (pp. 259-277). Buffalo, NY: International Center for Studies in Creativity.

Verganti, R. (2009). *Design-driven innovation: Changing the rules of competition by radically innovating what things mean.* Boston, MA: Harvard Business Press.

Wagner, D. G., & Berger, J. (1985). Do sociological theories grow? *American Journal of Sociology, 70,* 137-158.

Weick, K. E. (1995). *Sensemaking in organizations.* Thousand Oaks, CA: Sage Publications.

West, M. A., & Farr, J. L. (1990). Innovation at work. In M. A. West & J. L. Farr (Eds.), *Innovation and creativity at work: Psychological and organizational strategies* (pp. 3-13). Chichester, UK: Wiley.

Wheatley, W. J., Anthony, W. P., & Maddox, E. N. (1991). Selecting and training strategic planners with imagination and creativity. *Journal of Creative Behavior, 25*, 52-60.

Woodman, R. W. (2008). Creativity and organizational change: Linking ideas and extending theory. In J. Zhou & C. E. Shalley (Eds.). *Handbook of organizational creativity* (pp. 283-300). New York, NY: Lawrence Erlbaum Associates.

Woodman, R. W., Sawyer, J. E., & Griffin, R. W. (1993). Toward a theory of organizational creativity. *The Academy of Management Review, 18*(2), 293-321

Xu, F., & Rickards, T. (2007). Creative management: A predicted development from research into creativity and management. *Creativity and Innovation Management, 16*(3), 216-228.

About the Author

Andrés Mejía Villa is professor of strategic management and innovation at the University of La Sabana, Bogotá, Colombia. Currently, he is pursuing a doctoral degree in Economics and Management at the University of Navarra in Pamplona, Spain. His dissertation is titled, "The role of industry associations as drivers of strategic management of innovation in industry," through which he wants to understand the process of open innovation behind business associations as innovation intermediaries of their affiliated companies. His interest in innovation brought him to Buffalo State as a visiting scholar to deepen his understanding of the relationship between creativity and innovation at the organizational level. Andrés wishes to develop a model that integrates creativity and innovation, which he can then apply to a study of innovation intermediation phenomenon.

Email: andres.mejia@unisabana.edu.co, amejia@alumni.unav.es

How Can Organizations Motivate Employees Towards Creativity?

Celia Pillai
International Center for Studies in Creativity
SUNY Buffalo State

Abstract

This paper seeks to explore aspects of human motivation as they relate to creativity in an organizational context. Starting with a broad understanding of the fundamental drivers of human creative behavior, this paper explores factors influencing employee motivation for creativity. Key organizational mechanisms for motivating employees towards creativity are shown within a framework, and each of these are explored further. With its multiple influences and complexities, motivating employees for organizational creativity requires a nuanced understanding and a balanced application of variables like rewards, job design, group dynamics, goals, resources, evaluations, and leadership. More than 50 years of research has yielded many theories, constructs, and factors driving human motivation for creativity that contrast with the conventional approaches organizations widely employ. Implications for organizations and some future directions are discussed.

How Can Organizations Motivate Employees Towards Creativity?

W ay back in 1960, McGregor's book on employee motivation, *The Human Side of Enterprise,* challenged the prevalent "Theory X" with "Theory Y," based on different assumptions about human motivation. Theory X assumes employees are fundamentally passive and indolent; therefore, management's task is to direct employee efforts—motivating them, controlling their actions and modifying their behavior to fit organizational goals. Theory Y assumes employees are already motivated towards development and responsibility for organizational goals; thus, the task of management is to facilitate people to best achieve their own goals by directing their efforts towards organizational objectives. Years later, despite scientific evidence and understanding to the contrary, many organizations still seem to operate on the assumptions of Theory X. With this as a background, this paper looks at how organizational approaches drive—or do not drive—creative behavior in employees.

In an increasingly complex and dynamic world, creativity and innovation have become essential for organizations to thrive and grow. Yet, there is a widespread disconnect in understanding and applying the dynamics of what motivates employees towards creative behavior in organizations. When I reflect on my own experiences within organizations, I see how my motivation to be creative and produce creative outcomes varied significantly based on the existing organizational environment and motivational mechanisms. Instances when my creativity got killed were times when there was a mismatch between my own motivational orientation and the organizational assumptions. There remains a surprisingly large gap between theory and practice in this area. Fortunately, there is a wealth of knowledge available to help an organization tap into the creativity of its human resources, enabling it to make creative leaps into the future.

Creativity in an organizational context is a complex phenomenon involving multiple constituents, levels, and influences (Amabile, 1988, 1996; Woodman, Sawyer, & Griffin, 1993). Organizational creativity is essential for innovation—in fact, innovation happens on the bedrock of creativity. "Organizational creativity can be seen as a process where creativity is the input to the processes that lead to innovation, competitiveness and returns on investment" (Cook, 1998, p. 180). Research indicates that organizational creativity leads to tangible financial returns (Dyer, Gregersen, & Christensen, 2009; Geroski, Machin, & Van Reenen, 1993), employee value (Rasulzada & Dackert, 2009; Shalley, Gilson, &

Blum, 2000), competitive advantage (Florida & Goodnight, 2005), and growth in organizational capabilities (Basadur, 1997; Cook, 1998; Firestien, 1996).

And, where does an organization's creativity lie? As Simon (1965) put it succinctly, "The bulk of the productive wealth of our economy is not embedded in factories and machines but is to be found in the knowledge and skills stored in men's minds" (p. 71). Successful organizations know how to tap into the creative prowess of their people. Every innovation has its birth in the creativity of an individual or group. Many breakthrough ideas, products, and success stories have stemmed from employees' creative pursuits within organizations. Pontiac's Fiero automobile, the large electrostatic displays in Hewlett-Packard's instruments, *The Godfather,* 3M's tape slitter, and Light Emitting Diode (LED) bright lighting technology are just a few such examples (Mainemelis, 2010).

Organizational innovation requires people who are motivated to be creative. Amabile's (1988, 2012) componential model captures *task motivation* as one of the three primary components of organizational creativity. It is not capability but motivational orientation that decides what a creative individual will actually do in a given situation (Amabile, 1996). Motivation is not just an affective influence on creativity, but is also related to thinking and cognition (Runco & McGarva, 2013). Foundational to understanding the motivation for creativity in organizations is an appreciation of what drives creative behavior in human beings.

What Drives Creative Behavior in Humans?

The earliest modern psychology research linked the drive of creative behavior primarily to the direction of psychic energy. Freud (1958) viewed creativity as a means to fill one's repressed unconscious needs. This psychoanalytic view also saw creativity as being driven by the need to deal with the environment, feelings of efficacy, and voids in one's psychological make-up arising from past experiences (White, 1959). Jung (1960) looked at psychic energy in terms of the affective complexes that operate to store and release it. The role of psychic energy in creativity, especially as it related to attention, was later studied by others, including Csikszentmihalyi (1978) and Kahneman (1973). Many studies have also linked creativity to psychological troubles, psychopathology, and other mental illnesses (Arieti, 1976; Kaufman, 2001; Ludwig, 1995).

Maslow's (1943) landmark theory of human motivation views man as perpetually wanting. Within his hierarchy of needs (physiological, safety, love/belonging, esteem, and self-actualization), creativity was conceptualized at the highest level. Self-actualization is:

the desire to become more and more what one is, to become everything that one is capable of becoming.... It is not necessarily a creative urge although in people who have any capacities for creation it will take this form. (Maslow, 1943, p. 383)

Maslow (1943) suggested that the appearance of one need rests on the satisfaction of another, more "pre-potent" need. Thus, to be motivated for creativity requires a certain level of satisfaction of the other needs. But Maslow also cautioned that no drive can be treated as isolated or discrete: "Every drive is related to the state of satisfaction or dissatisfaction of other drives" (p. 370).

Other humanists such as Rogers (1954) concurred that creativity arises from individuals' exploration of their personal aptitudes and interests: "We must face the fact that the individual creates primarily because it is satisfying to him, because this behavior is felt to be self-actualizing" (p. 252). In this view, creativity arises from within an individual. The *psychoeconomic model* of creative process (Rubenson & Runco, 1992) looked at creative behavior in terms of costs and expected benefits—as a product of initial endowments and active investments in creative ability. Creative behavior is seen as a combination of internal and external factors and influences.

What are the Influences on Creative Behavior?

As shown in the previous section, creativity may be driven by dynamics of psychic energy, through investments in developing it, or as a higher-order need in man's eternal quest for expansion and self-actualization. The urge to be creative is a fundamental drive in humans. The intensity and level of activation of this drive may vary based on a complex set of influences that are at play.

Our understanding of the influences on creative behavior has evolved over the years to provide us with a fairly nuanced view of the subject. Early on, operant theorists believed that human behavior is controlled by external mechanisms—that it could be regulated using the associative relationships between consequence and behavior (Skinner, 1954). Behaviors were seen as being simply motivated by separable external consequences such as food or money. Hull's (1943) principles of behavior added physiological drive to this associative relationship. Behavior in these theories is assumed to be driven by past consequence based on the re- lationship between behavior and outcome. The widespread use of rewards and penalties in all walks of life is based on this assumption that human behavior can be best manipulated by rewarding for desirable behaviors and penalizing for undesirable ones—the classic carrot-and-stick approach used in workplaces.

Later theories laid emphasis on processing of information to determine value expectancy as an important aspect driving behavior. The psychological value of outcomes formed the primary basis, by comparing one's current state to a desired state and acting to reduce the gap between the two (Porter & Lawler, 1968). The focus here is on current and future consequences rather than the past. Deci and Ryan's (1985) *cognitive evaluation theory* was a major contribution in exploring motivations for creativity. It pointed out the role of one's perceptions of self-determination and competency for creativity to occur. Evolving to the broader *self-determination theory* (Deci & Ryan, 2008), it differentiated individual motivation orientations along three dimensions: autonomy, competence, and relatedness. This view looked at motivational orientation not as a universal phenomenon, but as person-specific. People vary not only in level of motivation but also in motivation orientation.

The extrinsic-intrinsic dimension of motivation has been a consistent theme in the inquiry into motivations of creative behavior (Amabile, 1990, 1996; Csikszentmihalyi, 1982; Hennessey, 2003). *Extrinsic motivation* is to be externally driven for a goal that is outside the task itself; for example, monetary reward for reaching a performance goal. *Intrinsic motivation,* in contrast, is to be internally driven to engage in an activity for its own sake; for example, when a person derives pleasure and enjoyment from an activity such as solving a difficult problem. While there are some differing views and results from studies on intrinsic motivation and its relationship to creativity, it is widely accepted as a key contributor in promoting creative behavior (Amabile, Hill, Hennessey, & Tighe, 1994; Dewett, 2007; Eisenberger & Aselage, 2009; Hannam & Narayan, 2015).

A dominance of informational factors (those that provide useful feedback) against controlling factors (those that convey external control) leads to greater intrinsic motivation and creativity as perception of external control is diminished (Deci & Ryan, 1985). Studies suggest that intrinsic motivation makes people curious, cognitively flexible, risk takers, persistent in the face of barriers, experience positive affect, and view their work environments as more fair (Hannam & Narayan, 2015; Silvia, 2008; Utman, 1997; Zhou & Shalley, 2003). In his popular book, Pink (2009) argued that human motivation is fundamentally intrinsic and is a function of autonomy, mastery, and purpose. Recent research also points to the influence of social networks, structures, and interactions within organizations on creativity (Jia, Shaw, Tsui, & Park, 2014; Perry-Smith & Shalley, 2014).

A considered view of these numerous, multi-dimensional, and complex influences in the design and application of motivational mechanisms will go a long way in promoting creativity in organizations.

What Levers Can Organizations Use to Motivate Creativity?

Despite mounting evidence to the contrary, many organizations continue to rely exclusively on carrot-and-stick approaches to influence employee behavior. While this approach may have legitimate uses, it is not the best method to drive creativity and innovation. I propose below a framework (Figure 1) that takes into consideration some of the major motivational mechanisms within organizations for creativity. This is followed by a brief exploration of each, informed by the discussions in the preceding sections and research into the specific areas.

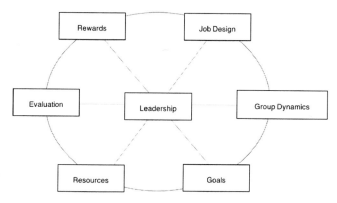

Figure 1: Motivational levers for organizational creativity

Rewards

Numerous studies have looked at the impact of reward, the most commonly-used motivator in organizations. Research indicates that rewards, inappropriately used, can kill intrinsic motivation and creativity (Amabile, 1996; Amabile, Hennessey, & Grossman, 1986; Deci, Koestner, & Ryan, 1999). But through a deeper understanding of their workings, rewards can be used positively for creativity. To assess their differing effects on creativity, Ryan, Mims, and Koestner (1983) used a distinction of reward-contingencies: *task-non-contingent rewards* (rewarding not for a specific task/activity, e.g., participation); *task-contingent rewards* (rewarding for a task/activity. e.g., completion of a task); and *performance-contingent rewards* (rewarding based on performance goals, e.g., a sales target). While task non-contingent and task-contingent rewards do not undermine intrinsic motivation, performance-contingent and *completion-contingent rewards* (rewarding based on task completion) significantly undermine it (Byron & Khazanchi, 2012; Deci et al., 1999), perhaps on account of the controlling component (Hennessey, 2000). The same holds true for measures on creativity (Selart, Nordström, Kuvaas, & Takemura, 2008). In a study looking at pay, Ramamoorthy, Flood, Slattery, and Sardessai (2005) found that "pay also had some modest effect in affecting innovative work behaviors" (p. 149). Using rewards positively for creativity calls for a nuanced understanding and clarity on the *what* (kind of reward), *how* (rewards are distributed), and *why* (the types of behaviors rewarded).

Job Design: Challenge, Autonomy, and Complexity

The way jobs are structured effects intrinsic motivation and creativity (Ohly & Fritz, 2010; Oldham & Cummings, 1996). Csikszentmihalyi (1990) described the concept of *flow* as an engrossing and phenomenological state when people engage in challenging tasks to their maximum ability. In this optimal state, one gives one's best and feels rewarded by the activity itself—like a peak state of intrinsic motivation. Finding the optimal match between challenge and skill is key here; thus, job structure is a contributor to intrinsic motivation and creativity of employees (Oldham & Cummings, 1996). For instance, challenge, autonomy, and complexity lead to focused attention and engagement (Shalley & Gilson, 2004). Challenge and complexity have been shown to give people excitement and a powerful sense of pleasure (Ohly & Fritz, 2010; Perkins, 1988). On autonomy, Collins and Amabile (1999) stated, "The freedom to choose what to work on allows individuals to seek out questions that they are highly intrinsically motivated to pursue. This high level of intrinsic interest will lay the groundwork for creative achievement" (p. 305). Many other studies, including the cognitive evaluation theory (Deci & Ryan, 1987), support this view:

> When autonomous, people experience themselves as initiators of their own behavior; they select desired outcomes and choose how to achieve them. Regulation through choice is characterized by flexibility and the absence of pressure. By contrast, being controlled is characterized by greater rigidity and the experience of having to do what one is doing. (p. 1025)

De Charms (1968) also included experiencing the satisfaction of the need for competence and autonomy as necessary for intrinsic motivation. Organizations need to provide for optimal levels of challenge, autonomy, complexity, and competence when designing roles that require high creativity.

Goals, Resource Availability, and Evaluation

Goal setting can be a very effective motivational technique to drive creative behavior (Amabile & Gryskiewicz, 1989; Locke & Latham, 1990). Specifying creativity goals leads to more creativity (Carson & Carson, 1993; Shalley, 1991, 1995), while emphasizing only performance goals has the opposite effect (Shalley, 1991). Clarity in organizational and creativity goals leads to greater creative outcomes from employees. People are motivated to act creatively when they know how they are contributing to a higher purpose or goal.

Apart from significant cognitive and affective investments, creativity needs an investment of time (Amabile, 1987). Some of the most innovative companies give employees dedicated time for pursuing creative ideas outside of their day-to-day job responsibilities; widely-reported examples include Google and 3M (Skarzynski & Gibson, 2013). Time awareness can help people give concrete form to their original ideas (Bissola & Imperatori, 2011). Creativity also requires a balance of material resources—not too constrained, yet not too abundant for the task at hand (Csikszentmihalyi, 1996).

Similar to the impact of rewards, evaluations have a complex influence on creativity. They can be dysfunctional to creativity (Amabile, Goldfarb, & Brackfleld, 1990; Shalley & Oldham, 1985), but when handled with care, can positively affect intrinsic motivation and creativity (Elliott & Harackiewicz, 1994; Jussim, Soffin, Brown, Ley, & Kohlhepp, 1992; Shalley, 1995). The mode, orientation, and delivery are important considerations in the design and deployment of evaluations to foster creativity. When evaluations are informational, supporting, and high on developmental orientation, creativity increases (Shalley & Perry-Smith, 2001; Zhou, 2003).

Group Dynamics and Collective Creativity

Creativity in organizations happens as a collective process—through collaboration by combining the knowledge, abilities, and skills of a diverse set of people. This has been a focus of research in recent times. For organizational creativity, moments of collective creativity are necessary (Hargadon & Bechky, 2006). There appears to be a positive correlation between individual and group creativity (Odoardi, Montani, Boudrias, & Battistelli, 2015; Pirola-Merlo & Mann, 2004; Taggar, 2002). When considering the dynamics of motivating collective creativity, organizational and social processes, as well as other-focused psychological processes, play important roles (Bissola & Imperatori, 2011; Grant & Berry, 2011). Prosocial motivation (focused on benefiting other people) strengthens the association between intrinsic motivation and creativity and is positively associated with adopting others' viewpoints to understand their preferences, values, and needs (Grant & Berry, 2011; Parker & Axtell, 2001). Amabile and Kramer (2011) identified the *nourishment factor* in team creativity—the different ways of providing interpersonal support, such as encouragement, respect, and collegiality. These findings point to the futility in the long-term of using competition as a motivational tool—especially so when creativity is the desired outcome. Competition may undermine creative thinking and innovation in organizations. The collective nature of organizational creativity is nurtured through collaboration and appropriate development of its social, cognitive and affective dimensions.

The Role of Leadership

Like a conductor of an orchestra, leadership plays an integrating role in motivating employees for creativity. Leaders create the symphony by balancing the various motivators and facilitating creative efforts by individuals and teams. Leader effectiveness is critical to the success of creative work in organizations (Redmond, Mumford, & Teach, 1993; Vinarski-Peretz & Carmeli, 2011). Leaders can play a positive role in creating the right roles, work environments, work relationships, and human resource practices such as rewards, goals, and evaluations. Zhang and Bartol (2010) found that empowering leadership positively affected psychological empowerment, which in turn influenced both intrinsic motivation and creative process engagement. Transformational leadership, a key concept in creative leadership, has been found to have a positive relationship to employee creativity (Gumusluoglu & Ilsev, 2009; Shin & Zhou, 2003). Avolio and Bass (1995) described transformational leadership as consisting of four components: charismatic role modeling, individualized consideration, inspirational motivation, and intellectual stimulation. On a similar note, Mumford, Scott, Gaddis, and Strange (2002) suggested "the leadership of creative efforts seems to call for an integrative style—a style that permits the leader to orchestrate expertise, people, and relationships in such a way as to bring new ideas into being" (p. 738). This anchoring role places leadership at the center of the framework suggested here (Figure 1).

Conclusions

Having reviewed a large number of studies on motivation for creativity, the most critical aspect that stands out to me is that of balance. Driving creative behavior requires a fine balance of multiple elements—individual and group motivations, extrinsic and intrinsic motivators, structure and flexibility, resource availability, and creative constraints. It also needs the right climate and leadership to facilitate this balance. None of the mechanisms (rewards, goals, resources, etc.) are categorically negative or positive for creativity, but through deeper understanding and proper usage, each of them can become powerful motivators. A word of caution here is to note that not all jobs require high levels of creativity, and the conventional Theory X (McGregor, 1960), with its carrot-and-stick approach, may still have its appropriate uses. Management first needs to be clear about their expectations of creativity from the various roles in the organization and then design and apply motivational mechanisms accordingly. Driving creativity and reaping its benefits requires a balanced application of motivational mechanisms, strong commitment, and a long-term view of outcomes.

The research so far on motivation for creativity has not delved into the intricacies of the different stages of the creative process. Since the creative process requires different cognitive and affective skills through its various stages (Puccio, Mance, & Murdock, 2011), the motivational implications under each of them can be examined. For example, rewards, goal setting, and time constraint may have differing dynamics during the idea generation stage as compared to the solution implementation stage of the creative process.

The intersection of motivation and creativity has varied complexities—including varied individual motivational orientations, differing effects and factors within motivational mechanisms, and the collective nature of organizational creativity. With the current base of research on several different dimensions, possible next steps include developing an integrated view using the best of different theories, understanding the underlying dynamics of some of the contradictory findings, and a cross-pollination of different contexts (e.g., applied research in education could be validated for organizations and vice-versa). While there is ongoing research on the motivational nuances due to the collective nature of organizational creativity, much work still remains in understanding these dynamics within groups and how they interweave with the dynamics of individuals. The most pertinent question that remains is how to integrate theory and practice in organizations by widely applying the understanding we have available. A rigorous focus on using an applied approach to future research in the field may perhaps be a step toward this end.

References

Amabile, T. (1987). The motivation to be creative. In S. Isaksen (Ed.), *Frontiers of Creativity Research: Beyond the basics* (pp. 223-254). Buffalo, NY: Bearly Limited.

Amabile, T. M. (1988). A model of creativity and innovation in organizations. In B. M. Staw & L. L. Cummings (Eds.), *Research in organizational behavior* (Vol. 10, pp. 123-167). Greenwich, CT: JAI Press.

Amabile, T. M. (1990). Within you, without you: The social psychology of creativity, and beyond. In M. A. Runco & R. S. Albert (Eds.), *Theories of Creativity* (pp. 61-91). Newbury Park, CA: Sage Publications.

Amabile, T. M. (1996, January). *Creativity and innovation in organizations.* Harvard Business School Background Note 396-239. Retrieved from http://www.hbs.edu/faculty/Pages/item.aspx?num=13672

Amabile, T. M. (2012, May 12). *Componential theory of creativity.* Harvard Business School Working Paper Number 12-096. Retrieved from http://hbswk.hbs.edu/item/componential-theory-of-creativity

Amabile, T. M., Goldfarb, P., & Brackfleld, S. C. (1990). Social influences on creativity: Evaluation, coaction, and surveillance. *Creativity Research Journal, 3*(1), 6-21.

Amabile, T. M., & Gryskiewicz, N. D. (1989). The creative environment scales: Work environment inventory. *Creativity Research Journal, 2*(4), 231-253.

Amabile, T. M., Hennessey, B. A., & Grossman, B. S. (1986). Social influences on creativity: The effects of contracted-for reward. *Journal of Personality and Social Psychology, 50*(1), 14-23.

Amabile, T. M., Hill, K. G., Hennessey, B. A., & Tighe, E. M. (1994). The Work Preference Inventory: Assessing intrinsic and extrinsic motivational orientations. *Journal of Personality and Social Psychology, 66*(5), 950.

Amabile, T., & Kramer, S. (2011). *The progress principle: Using small wins to ignite joy, engagement, and creativity at work.* Boston, MA: Harvard Business Review Press.

Arieti, S. (1976). *Creativity: The magic synthesis.* New York, NY: Basic Books.

Atkinson, J. W. (1957). Motivational determinants of risk-taking behavior. *Psychological Review, 64*(6, pt.1), 359-372.

Avolio, B. J., & Bass, B. M. (1995). Individual consideration viewed at multiple levels of analysis: A multi-level framework for examining the diffusion of transformational leadership. *The Leadership Quarterly, 6*(2), 199-218.

Basadur, M. (1997). Organizational development interventions for enhancing creativity in the workplace. *Journal of Creative Behavior, 31*(1), 59-72.

Bissola, R., & Imperatori, B. (2011). Organizing individual and collective creativity: Flying in the face of creativity clichés. *Creativity and Innovation Management, 20*(2), 77-89.

Byron, K., & Khazanchi, S. (2012). Rewards and creative performance: A meta-analytic test of theoretically derived hypotheses. *Psychological Bulletin, 138*(4), 809-830.

Carson, P. P., & Carson, K. D. (1993). Managing creativity enhancement through goal-setting and feedback. *Journal of Creative Behavior, 27*(1), 36-45.

Collins, M. A., & Amabile, T. M. (1999). Motivation and creativity. In R. J. Sternberg (Ed.), *Handbook of creativity* (pp. 297-312). Cambridge, UK: Cambridge University Press.

Cook, P. (1998). The creativity advantage: Is your organization the leader of the pack? *Industrial and Commercial Training, 30*(5), 179-184.

Csikszentmihalyi, M. (1978). Attention and the holistic approach to behavior. In K. S. Pope & J. L. Singer (Eds.), *The stream of consciousness* (pp. 335-358). New York, NY: Plenum.

Csikszentmihalyi, M. (1982). Toward a psychology of optimal experience. In L. Wheeler (Ed.), *Review of personality and social psychology* (Vol. 2, pp. 13-36). Beverly Hills, CA: Sage Publications.

Csikszentmihalyi, M. (1990). *Flow: The psychology of optimal experience.* New York, NY: Cambridge University Press.

Csikszentmihalyi, M. (1996). *Creativity: Flow and the psychology of discovery and invention.* New York, NY: HarperPerennial.

de Charms, R. (1968). *Personal causation: The internal affective determinants of behavior.* New York, NY: Academic Press.

Deci, E. L., Koestner, R., & Ryan, R. M. (1999). A meta-analytic review of experiments examining the effects of extrinsic rewards on intrinsic motivation. *Psychological Bulletin, 125*(6), 627-668.

Deci, E. L., & Ryan, R. (1985). *Intrinsic motivation and self-determination in human behavior.* New York, NY: Plenum.

Deci, E. L., & Ryan, R. M. (1987). The support of autonomy and the control of behavior. *Journal of Personality and Social Psychology, 53*(6), 1024-1037.

Deci, E. L., & Ryan, R. M. (2008). Self-determination theory: A macrotheory of human motivation, development, and health. *Canadian Psychology/ Psychologie Canadienne, 49*(3), 182-185.

Dewett, T. (2007). Linking intrinsic motivation, risk taking, and employee creativity in an R&D environment. *R&D Management, 37*(3), 197-208.

Dyer, J. H., Gregersen, H. B., & Christensen, C. M. (2009). The innovator's DNA. *Harvard Business Review, 87*(12), 60-67.

Eisenberger, R., & Aselage, J. (2009). Incremental effects of reward on experienced performance pressure: Positive outcomes for intrinsic interest and creativity. *Journal of Organizational Behavior, 30*(1), 95-117.

Elliot, A. J., & Harackiewicz, J. M. (1994). Goal setting, achievement orientation, and intrinsic motivation: A mediational analysis. *Journal of Personality and Social Psychology, 66*(5), 968-980.

Firestien, R. (1996). *Leading on the creative edge: Gaining competitive advantage through the power of creative problem solving.* Colorado Springs, CO: Piñon Press.

Florida, R., & Goodnight, J. (2005). Managing for creativity. *Harvard Business Review, 83*(7), 124-131.

Freud, S. (1958). *On creativity and the unconscious: Papers on the psychology of art, literature, love, religion.* New York, NY: Harper.

Geroski, P., Machin, S., & Van Reenen, J. (1993). The profitability of innovating firms. *RAND Journal of Economics, 24*(2) 198-211.

Grant, A. M., & Berry, J. W. (2011). The necessity of others is the mother of invention: Intrinsic and prosocial motivations, perspective taking, and creativity. *Academy of Management Journal, 54*(1), 73-96.

Gumusluoglu, L., & Ilsev, A. (2009). Transformational leadership, creativity, and organizational innovation. *Journal of Business Research, 62*(4), 461-473.

Hannam, K., & Narayan, A. (2015). Intrinsic motivation, organizational justice, and creativity. *Creativity Research Journal, 27*(2), 214-224.

Hargadon, A. B., & Bechky, B. A. (2006). When collections of creatives become creative collectives: A field study of problem solving at work. *Organization Science, 17*(4), 484-500.

Hennessey, B. A. (2000). Rewards and creativity. In C. Sansone & J. Harackiewicz (Eds.), *Intrinsic and extrinsic motivation: The search for optimal motivation and performance* (pp. 55-78). New York, NY: Academic Press.

Hennessey, B. A. (2003). The social psychology of creativity. *Scandinavian Journal of Educational Research, 47*(3), 253-271.

Hull, C. (1943). *Principles of behavior: An introduction to behavior theory.* Oxford, England: Appleton-Century-Crofts.

Jia, L., Shaw, J. D., Tsui, A. S., & Park, T. Y. (2014). A social–structural perspective on employee-organization relationships and team creativity. *Academy of Management Journal, 57*(3), 869-891.

Jung, C. G. (1960). On psychic energy. *The collected works of Carl Jung* (Vol. 8, pp. 3-66). Princeton, NJ: Princeton University Press.

Jussim, L., Soffin, S., Brown, R., Ley, J., & Kohlhepp, K. (1992). Understanding reactions to feedback by integrating ideas from symbolic interactionism and cognitive evaluation theory. *Journal of Personality and Social Psychology, 62*(3), 402-421.

Kahneman, D. (1973). *Attention and effort.* Englewood Cliffs, NJ: Prentice-Hall.

Kaufman, J. C. (2001). The Sylvia Plath effect: Mental illness in eminent creative writers. *Journal of Creative Behavior, 35*(1), 37-50.

Locke, E., & Latham, G. (1990). *A theory of goal setting & task performance.* Englewood Cliffs, NJ: Prentice Hall.

Ludwig, A. (1995). *The price of greatness: Resolving the creativity and madness controversy.* New York, NY: Guilford Press.

Mainemelis, C. (2010). Stealing fire: Creative deviance in the evolution of new ideas. *Academy of Management Review, 35*(4), 558-578.

Maslow, A. H. (1943). A theory of human motivation. *Psychological Review, 50*(4), 370-396.

McGregor, D. (1960). *The human side of enterprise.* New York, NY: McGraw-Hill.

Mumford, M. D., Scott, G. M., Gaddis, B., & Strange, J. M. (2002). Leading creative people: Orchestrating expertise and relationships. *The Leadership Quarterly, 13*(6), 705-750.

Odoardi, C., Montani, F., Boudrias, J. S., & Battistelli, A. (2015). Linking managerial practices and leadership style to innovative work behavior: The role of group and psychological processes. *Leadership & Organization Development Journal, 36*(5), 545-569.

Ohly, S., & Fritz, C. (2010). Work characteristics, challenge appraisal, creativity, and proactive behavior: A multi-level study. *Journal of Organizational Behavior, 31*(4), 543-565.

Oldham, G. R., & Cummings, A. (1996). Employee creativity: Personal and contextual factors at work. *Academy of Management Journal, 39*(3), 607-634.

Parker, S. K., & Axtell, C. M. (2001). Seeing another viewpoint: Antecedents and outcomes of employee perspective taking. *Academy of Management Journal, 44*(6), 1085-1100.

Perkins, D. N. (1988). The possibility of invention. In R. J. Sternberg (Ed.), *The nature of creativity* (pp. 362-385). Cambridge, UK: Cambridge University Press.

Perry-Smith, J. E., & Shalley, C. E. (2014). A social composition view of team creativity: The role of member nationality-heterogeneous ties outside of the team. *Organization Science, 25*(5), 1434-1452.

Pink, D. (2009). *Drive: The surprising truth about what motivates us.* New York, NY: Riverhead Books.

Pirola-Merlo, A., & Mann, L. (2004). The relationship between individual creativity and team creativity: Aggregating across people and time. *Journal of Organizational Behavior, 25*(2), 235-257.

Porter, L., & Lawler, E. (1968). *Managerial attitudes and performance.* Homewood, IL: R.D. Irwin.

Puccio, G. P., Mance, M., & Murdock, M. C. (2011). *Creative leadership: Skills that drive change* (2nd ed.). Thousand Oaks, CA: Sage Publications.

Ramamoorthy, N., Flood, P. C., Slattery, T., & Sardessai, R. (2005). Determinants of innovative work behavior: Development and test of an integrated model. *Creativity and Innovation Management, 14*(2), 142-150.

Rasulzada, F., & Dackert, I. (2009). Organizational creativity and innovation in relation to psychological well-being and organizational factors. *Creativity Research Journal, 21*(2-3), 191-198.

Redmond, M. R., Mumford, M. D., & Teach, R. (1993). Putting creativity to work: Effects of leader behavior on subordinate creativity. *Organizational Behavior and Human Decision Processes, 55*(1), 120-151.

Rogers, C. R. (1954). Toward a theory of creativity. *ETC: A Review of General Semantics, 11*, 249-260.

Rubenson, D. L., & Runco, M. A. (1992). The psychoeconomic approach to creativity. *New Ideas in Psychology, 10*(2), 131-147.

Runco, M. A., & McGarva, D. I. (2013). Creativity and motivation. In S. Kreitler (Ed.), *Cognition and motivation: Forging an interdisciplinary perspective* (pp. 468-482). Cambridge, UK: Cambridge University Press.

Ryan, R. M., Mims, V., & Koestner, R. (1983). Relation of reward contingency and interpersonal context to intrinsic motivation: A review and test using cognitive evaluation theory. *Journal of Personality and Social Psychology, 45*(4), 736-750.

Selart, M., Nordström, T., Kuvaas, B., & Takemura, K. (2008). Effects of reward on self-regulation, intrinsic motivation and creativity. *Scandinavian Journal of Educational Research, 52*(5), 439-458.

Shalley, C. E. (1991). Effects of productivity goals, creativity goals, and personal discretion on individual creativity. *Journal of Applied Psychology, 76*(2), 179-185.

Shalley, C. E. (1995). Effects of coaction, expected evaluation, and goal setting on creativity and productivity. *Academy of Management Journal, 38*(2), 483-503.

Shalley, C. E., & Gilson, L. L. (2004). What leaders need to know: A review of social and contextual factors that can foster or hinder creativity. *The Leadership Quarterly, 15*(1), 33-53.

Shalley, C. E., Gilson, L. L., & Blum, T. C. (2000). Matching creativity requirements and the work environment: Effects on satisfaction and intentions to leave. *Academy of Management Journal, 43*(2), 215-223.

Shalley, C. E., & Oldham, G. R. (1985). Effects of goal difficulty and expected external evaluation on intrinsic motivation: A laboratory study. *Academy of Management Journal, 28*(3), 628-640.

Shalley, C. E., & Perry-Smith, J. E. (2001). Effects of social-psychological factors on creative performance: The role of informational and controlling expected evaluation and modeling experience. *Organizational Behavior and Human Decision Processes, 84*(1), 1-22.

Shin, S. J., & Zhou, J. (2003). Transformational leadership, conservation, and creativity: Evidence from Korea. *Academy of Management Journal, 46*(6), 703-714.

Silvia, P. J. (2008). Interest: The curious emotion. *Current Directions in Psychological Science, 17*(1), 57-60.

Simon, H. A. (1965). *Administrative behavior* (Vol. 4). New York, NY: Free Press.

Skarzynski, P., & Gibson, R. (2013). *Innovation to the core: A blueprint for transforming the way your company innovates.* Boston, MA: Harvard Business Review Press.

Skinner, B. F. (1954). The science of learning and the art of teaching. *Harvard Educational Review, 24*, 86-97.

Taggar, S. (2002). Individual creativity and group ability to utilize individual creative resources: A multilevel model. *Academy of Management Journal, 45*(2), 315-330.

Utman, C. H. (1997). Performance effects of motivational state: A meta-analysis. *Personality and Social Psychology Review, 1*(2), 170-182.

Vinarski-Peretz, H., & Carmeli, A. (2011). Linking care felt to engagement in innovative behaviors in the workplace: The mediating role of psychological conditions. *Psychology of Aesthetics, Creativity, and the Arts, 5*(1), 43-53.

White, R. W. (1959). Motivation reconsidered: The concept of competence. *Psychological Review, 66*(5), 297-333.

Woodman, R. W., Sawyer, J. E., & Griffin, R. W. (1993). Toward a theory of organizational creativity. *Academy of Management Review, 18*(2), 293-321.

Zhang, X., & Bartol, K. M. (2010). Linking empowering leadership and employee creativity: The influence of psychological empowerment, intrinsic motivation, and creative process engagement. *Academy of Management Journal, 53*(1), 107-128.

Zhou, J. (2003). When the presence of creative coworkers is related to creativity: Role of supervisor close monitoring, developmental feedback, and creative personality. *Journal of Applied Psychology, 88*(3), 413-422.

Zhou, J., & Shalley, C. E. (2003). Research on employee creativity: A critical review and directions for future research. *Research in Personnel and Human Resources Management, 22*, 165-217.

About the Author

Celia Pillai is an executive strategy consultant and creativity and innovation specialist from India. She brings together her rich insights and experiences in business strategy, design thinking and creativity into her engagements with organizations and institutions. In her corporate experience spanning a decade at IBM, Celia has led multiple strategy and transformation projects in India and growth markets around the world. A qualified architect with a B.Arch. from Bangalore University, India, she has a range of design experiences. Celia also has a PGDM/MBA from Indian Institute of Management, Indore, India, and an M.S. in Creativity from SUNY Buffalo State. Combined with a passion to ignite human creativity, her rich and varied experiences bring together a unique blend of skills that intersect design and business strategy on a solid foundation in the science of creativity and innovation.

email: celia@creativiti.in
website: www.creativiti.in

Collaborative Problem Solving: What Helps or Hinders its Usefulness in Creative Efforts?

Diane R. Bessel, PhD, LMSW, CNM
International Center for Studies in Creativity
SUNY Buffalo State

Abstract

Interest in collaborative problem solving—the act of engaging diverse people to develop and/or deliver products, goods, or services beyond the scope of individual actors—has increased dramatically over the past several decades. Yet, despite this interest and the ample evidence of collaborative problem solving's many benefits, many professionals express frustration and experience challenges in their efforts to maximize its creative potential. This paper examines the literature from various disciplines including management, psychology, social work, sociology, health care, planning, and creativity to identify factors that help or hinder collaborative problem solving. Particular attention is paid to four key capacities deemed critical for effectively using this technique: individual capacity (including member characteristics, abilities, and skills); relational capacity (including communication, boundary spanning, shared vision and goals, and shared decision making); environmental capacity (including developing an appropriate culture and structure for collaborative endeavors); and organizational capacity (including organizational leadership and other support for problem solving).

Collaborative Problem Solving: What Helps or Hinders its Usefulness in Creative Efforts?

Interest in collaborative problem solving—the act of engaging diverse people to develop and/or deliver products, goods, or services beyond the scope of individual actors—has increased dramatically over the past several decades in a wide range of societal sectors (Thompson, 2013).

Within the business sector, group-based collaborations are frequently used to enhance innovation, particularly when bringing a new product or service to market (Sawyer, 2012). In academia, evidence suggests that, when compared with individual researchers, collaborative teams have generated more highly cited (i.e., more influential) research in every area over the past fifty years (Wuchty, Jones, & Uzzi, 2007). Consequently, major research funders, including the National Science Foundation and the National Institutes of Health, have begun to focus their resources on team-based efforts (Wuchty et. al, 2007). Within the public and non-profit sectors, collaborative efforts are increasingly viewed as critical to the delivery of health and human services in light of increased demands (e.g., consumer, regulatory, and time-pressure); and vanguard organizations, such as the Institute of Medicine, have called for "collaborative system change" to align public health, health care, and community services (Ansari, Philips, & Zwi, 2004; Leavitt & Lipman-Blumen, 1995; Sowa, 2008).

Evidence suggests there are myriad benefits for those who are able to solve problems collaboratively, including opportunities for greater creativity, increased energy for action, and greater access to a broad array of resources (Conoley & Conoley, 2010; Notgarnie, 2011; Sawyer, 2007; Thompson 2013). Positive collaborations are also said to expand the competence of the persons directly involved and may even penetrate beyond these initial relationships to modify the nature of engagement between groups, teams, and organizations (Bruusgaard, Pinto, Swindle, & Yoshino, 2010; Dovidio, Saguy, & Shnabel, 2009; Sowa, 2008).

Many organizations engaged in collaboration are able to improve their service delivery, efficiency, and public value-creating opportunities for securing additional financial resources for future endeavors (Sowa, 2008). Overall, successful collaborations often result in greater satisfaction and/or fewer complaints among customers and clientele; higher quality and greater continuity of care (especially in clinical settings); more efficient use of time; reduced fragmentation; improved working relationships; greater job satisfaction; improved outcomes; and cost reductions (Bruner, Waite, & Davey, 2011; Dovidio et al., 2009; Lasker, Weiss, & Miller, 2001; Mitchell, Parker, Giles, & White, 2010).

Yet, despite the push towards collaboration and the research that suggests its value, many professionals continue to hold a negative view of collaboration—and the weight of evidence suggests that this more pessimistic outlook might also be valid (Hudson, 2007). Collaboration is often hindered by traditional professionalism, which emphasizes individual decision making and accountability; disciplinary boundaries and identities (especially in relation to knowledge, standards, and terminology); and disparate cultures often based on department or task (Mulvale & Bourgeault, 2007; Perrault, McClelland, Austin, & Sieppert, 2011; Thompson, 2013).

These "older" models of professionalism can be difficult to overcome and typically produce poor outcomes when associated with collaborative problem solving efforts (Dovidio et al., 2009; Hudson, 2007). This leaves many professionals frustrated and unable to tap into the creative potential of this technique. Further, evidence suggests that collaboration does not simply occur because administration or management mandates that it be so. Instead, collaboration can only be sustained through the appropriate use of knowledge and skills among professionals as well as the ability to develop and maintain relationships that include trust, mutual understanding, and regard for one another (Friend, 2000; Thompson, 2013).

This paper seeks to broaden the understanding of collaborative problem solving and to provide insight as to what helps or hinders its usefulness in creative efforts. It draws on scholarly literature from various disciplines including management, psychology, social work, sociology, health care, and planning with a special emphasis on creativity research.

In Context

Sawyer (2012) indicated that the past 30 years have seen a tremendous growth in research on organizational innovation. Nevertheless, researchers have only very recently (i.e., since the 1990s) begun to investigate the role of collaboration—especially as it relates to creative groups.

Literature on group creativity focuses on two broad approaches: *input-output* and *process* (Sawyer, 2012). Input-output (IO) approaches examine how various inputs—including group composition, leadership, task design, competition, or environment—effect outcomes such as effectiveness or efficiency. Process approaches seek to understand observed relations between inputs and outputs by examining group development, decision-making processes, and flow.

While the research literature on the role of groups in creative efforts is still fairly nascent, there is a good deal of clarity about groups' potential, especially as it relates to solving complex and/or difficult problems. Schwartz (1995) found that groups typically outperform a comparable number of individuals when problems involve three-dimensional spatial information and transformation. Groups also tend to do the same on problems that require an understanding of verbal, numeric, or logical conceptual systems (Laughlin, Hatch, Silver, & Boh, 2006). Finally, cognitively diverse groups are more likely to solve ambiguous problems, including those problems that are not well understood or problems that need to be formulated by their members (Sawyer, 2012).

Regarding the look of collaborative problem solving groups, it appears that they can take on varied forms. Sawyer (2007, 2012) found that group innovation does not follow a "typical" linear developmental sequence as suggested by Tuckman (1965), but, rather, occurs iteratively; and similarly, that group innovation can occur over time through a constant series of small insights that accumulate and result in creative outcomes. Sawyer (2007, 2012) also found that ideas and strategies originate from the "bottom up" through self-managing groups that are not dominated by a single individual but involve all members.

Sawyer and DeZutter (2009) also introduced the idea of *collaborative emergence*, which is found when there is little or no structured plan or leadership guiding a group's discussions and/or behaviors. Accordingly, groups can be highly im-provisational—like jazz ensembles, improv theater, or children's fantasy play. Collaborative emergence, however, requires four important characteristics: it is based on an egalitarian ethos wherein everyone can contribute; it lacks specificity, intentionally allowing members to make sense and build meaning together; it is based in moment-to-moment transactions, which create unlimited options based on high levels of acceptance among group members; and it engages retroactive meaning, where meaning is made clear only through the contributions of others (Sawyer, 2010; Sawyer & DeZutter, 2009).

In contrast, Thompson (2013) noted that when group collaborations are conscious, planned, and focused on generating new or novel ideas, they can develop into what she described as a "creative conspiracy" (which served as the title of her book). In Thompson's view, teams that "conspire" organize themselves, motivate one another, and combine their talents to commit creative and innovative acts. Such acts are considered the hallmark of highly successful organizations.

Helping and Hindering

While collaborative problem solving groups can take on various forms, there are several factors that help or hinder the underlying processes involved. These factors can be grouped into four core capacities.* *Individual capacity* focuses on the individual characteristics, abilities, and skills needed to engage in collaborative problem solving. *Relational capacity* centers on the ability of group members to develop relationships that are rooted in trust and inclusiveness while also uniting around a shared vision and decision-making process. *Environmental capacity* describes the nature of the group's culture and structure. *Organizational capacity* describes the importance of strong leadership and additional supports for the collaborative problem solving process. These will be discussed in turn.

Individual Capacity

Individual capacity highlights several characteristics, abilities, and skills held by members of highly successful collaborative efforts.

Individual characteristics. Research suggests several characteristics are favored among members of collaborative efforts. These include honesty, integrity, reliability, competence, empathy, flexibility, responsibility, accountability, coordination, communication, assertiveness, autonomy, mutual trust and respect, and a sense of humor (Bruusgaard et al., 2010). Strong collaborators are generally self-aware, reciprocal in nature, willing to share and receive information, and highly adaptable (Thomson & Perry, 2006). They are also comfortable in the role of both leader and follower and readily bring fresh ideas, approaches, and perspectives to problems (Hudson, 2007).

Individual abilities. To maximize creativity and synergy, group members must be willing and able to share credit for the group's accomplishments; to create a common language of key concepts; and to recruit other members with similar characteristics. Members must also possess the ability to move away from limiting, predefined roles in order to think about their work in creative and holistic ways (Lasker et al., 2001; Thomson & Perry, 2006). They must also possess the ability to consider individual and organizational self-interests and to accept that all participants have a legitimate stake in the collaborative effort (Bridges, Davidson, Odegard, Maki, & Tomkowiak, 2011; Chizhik, Shelly, & Troyer, 2009).

---

*These capacities are loosely based on a study of community collaboration conducted by Bayne-Smith, Mizrahi, and Garcia (2008).

Whenever possible, member motives should be matched or at least understood and found to be complementary (rather than conflicting) prior to the start of a collaborative effort. Likewise, members must believe in the legitimacy of the effort ("buy-in") as well as hold and maintain a positive attitude about their roles in the collaborative effort (Leavitt & Lipman-Blumen, 1995).

Individual skills. In order to be effective in collaborative problem solving, it is critical that individuals possess key skills related to facilitation and organization (Thompson, 2013). Of particular concern is the ability to effectively manage typical idea-generating activities such as brainstorming, a technique that relies on deferral of judgment and large quantities of ideas. There are a number of factors that make brainstorming less effective in collaborative settings (Sawyer, 2012; Thompson, 2013). These include *motivation losses* in which group members begin to "free ride" on the contributions of others rather than provide their own input, and *coordination losses* in which group members engage in self-censorship or prejudge the quality of their own contributions and resist voicing all of their ideas to the group (Sawyer, 2012; Thompson, 2013). To address these concerns, group members must be well trained and may benefit from specified performance goals and clear criteria for "good ideas" (Sawyer, 2012).

Relational Aspects

Relational capacity centers on the ability of the group to develop relationships that are rooted in trust and inclusiveness while also uniting around shared vision and decision making. These activities require strong communication as well as the ability of members to engage with one another in collaborative problem solving activities.

Communication. One of the most common factors in the success or failure of collaborative problem solving is communication. O'Daniel and Rosenstein (2008) described several communication areas of particular importance, including: a clear sense of direction for the group; clear roles and tasks; acknowledgment and processing of conflict; clear specifications regarding authority and accountability; clear decision-making procedures; uniformity in access to resources; an emphasis on regular group evaluation (process and outcomes); and a willingness to make adjustments to the group based on evaluation.

Boundary spanning. Research on highly successful collaborative efforts also highlights the importance of *boundary spanning,* a term used to describe the ability of team members to understand differing perspectives, as well as those who are comfortable with sharing ideas, resources, and power. Boundary spanners are frequently the coordinators of group activity and primary negotiators of group conflict. They also bring about opportunities for group engagement.

Boundary spanners often possess an entrepreneurial-like ability to cultivate relationships using small but vital behind-the-scenes activities to build relationships (Miller, 2008). They also possess a strong allegiance to the group as well as to their own interests, which empowers them to move freely among group members in an effort to make relationships harmonious and productive (Morse, 2010). Boundary spanners play a critical role in collaborative efforts as they bring superior diplomacy and mediation skills (Nissen, 2010).

Shared vision and goals. In order for collaboration to succeed, members must balance individual, organizational, and collective concerns while reconciling their allegiance to and identification with various interested parties (Glaser, Bruckner, & Bannon, 2010; Takahashi & Smutny, 2001). This is particularly important as group identification may trigger rivalry and conflict related to these varied interests (Richter, West, van Dick, & Dawson, 2006). Understanding how to navigate this conflict is critical to group success (Notgarnie, 2011; Thomson & Perry, 2006).

Whenever possible, collaborative members should take part in the development of unified vision and goals. Doing so can help the group create a shared belief in the potential found in working together. This can also serve as a tool used to mediate intragroup conflict (Ansari et al., 2004; Chizhik et al., 2009). Similarly, rules should be created jointly and used to hold members accountable to ensure that all group members are treated as equals. Failure to do so can be catastrophic for group functioning (Thomson & Perry, 2006).

Shared decision making. Shared decision making is also critical, particularly when power differentials exist among group members based on education, title, position, or length of experience. Group members must have clear roles and must have the ability to provide input in all aspects of group decision making (Thomson & Perry, 2006). Knowledge of history and previous interactions among and between collaborative partners is also crucial. Finally, the group should emphasize open communication, acceptance, trust, respect, empathy for and among members, and understanding (Perrault et al., 2011).

Environmental Capacity

Environmental capacity describes the nature of the culture and structure developed by the various members of a collaborative effort.

Culture. A culture of openness and support among members is critical to collaborative problem solving efforts. Members need to build relationships based on mutual respect and their shared commitment to a successful collaboration (Leavitt & Lipman-Blumen, 1995; Milstein, Manierre, Susman, & Bruce,

2008). Collaboration is largely about respect, and only when all team members are supported through coordinated and cooperative efforts will participants be willing and able to maintain their interactions with one another (Friend, 2000).

Notably, groups often focus on commonalities rather than differences (Hudson, 2007). As a result, issues of diversity and related power differentials, inequalities, or oppression can be especially challenging for collaborative efforts. Here, diversity can be viewed as beneficial or detrimental depending on how it is handled within the group. It can lead to the generation of a wider range of ideas or it can damage group satisfaction and larger group processes (Chizhik et al., 2009; Leavitt & Lipman-Blumen, 1995).

Collaborators should seek to acknowledge and understand differences among group members especially in relation to disciplines, roles, statuses, and cultures (Bayne-Smith et al., 2008; Reich & Reich, 2006). Special efforts should be made to understand individual differences and to seek out diverse opinions as a core component of the group's culture. In order to promote positive outcomes, collaborative groups should engage in regular assessments of group processes and should also seek to increase sensitivity to one another, especially in relation to group dynamics (Reich & Reich, 2006).

Structure. Finally, group structure also has a significant effect on collaborative success (Dovidio et al., 2009). While clear group structures contribute to effectiveness and help to solidify group structure and direction, they are also often tied to hierarchical decision making and group structures (Dovidio et al., 2009; O'Daniel & Rosenstein, 2008).

The development of a hierarchy can lead to the development of subgroups and inequality among members. When faced with inequality in a group setting, disadvantaged members are more likely to act in favor of change, while advantaged groups members are more likely to act in favor of stability. To avoid this concern, collaborative groups should seek out opportunities to develop a consensus-based structure and to eschew hierarchy whenever possible.

In addition, group structures must also be non-punitive and must enable all members to engage freely in problem-solving efforts. Leveling inequalities may result in a short-term loss of order or more frequent conflict, but it can also lead to a greater expression of minority opinions. If conflict is received openly, it can effectively contribute to group development, enabling the group to develop a stronger product, good, or service (Dovidio et al., 2009).

Organizational Capacity

Finally, organizational capacity requires strong leadership and additional supports for the collaborative problem solving process.

Organizational leadership. Lack of understanding about the nature of collaborative efforts among organizational management can severely undermine a group's effectiveness from the outset (Friend, 2000). In contrast, an organization's administration can facilitate efficiency and efficacy by allowing room for spontaneity; encouraging intellectual intensity, integrity, and curiosity; valuing truth; helping to break down barriers; and selecting talented people to participate in collaborative problem solving activities (Leavitt & Lipman-Blumen, 1995).

Other organizational barriers. Other noted organizational barriers to collaborative practice include lack of stable and long-term funding; lack of functional organization within and between agencies; service gaps; frequent staff turnover; and differing practice styles and training among key staff members (Chizhik et al., 2009; Mulvale & Bourgeault, 2007).

Conclusion

Future research should continue to examine the important role that groups play in facilitating the development of creative ideas and strategies through collaborative problem solving. Researchers may be particularly interested in continuing to examine the characteristics of strong collaborators, as well as the nature of collaborative relationships within various settings. Additionally, they may be interested in determining which environments and organizational structures are most favorable for collaborative problem solving. Finally, researchers should also consider the long-term effectiveness of group problem-solving approaches vis-à-vis other efforts.

References

Ansari, W., Philips, C., & Zwi, A. (2004). Public health nurses' perspectives on collaborative partnerships in South Africa. *Public Health Nursing, 21*(3), 277-286.

Bayne-Smith, M., Mizrahi, T., & Garcia, M. (2008). Interdisciplinary community collaboration: Perspectives of community practitioners on successful strategies. *Journal of Community Practice, 16*(3), 249-269. doi:10.1080/10705420802255122

Bridges, D. R., Davidson, R. A., Odegard, P. S., Maki, I. V., & Tomkowiak, J. (2011). Interprofessional collaboration: Three best practice models of interprofessional education. *Medical Education Online, 16,* 10.3402/meo. v16i0.6035.

Bruner, P., Waite, R., & Davey, M. P. (2011). Providers' perspectives on collaboration. *International Journal of Integrated Care, 11*(31), 1-11.

Bruusgaard, E., Pinto, P., Swindle, J., & Yoshino, S. (2010). "Are we all on the same page?": The challenges and charms of collaboration on a journey through interdisciplinarity. *Graduate Journal of Social Sciences, 7*(1), 39-58.

Chizhik, A. W., Shelly, R. K., & Troyer, L. (2009). Intragroup conflict and cooperation: An introduction. *Journal of Social Issues, 62*(2), 251-259.

Conoley, J., & Conoley, C. (2010). Why does collaboration work? Linking positive psychology and collaboration. *Journal of Educational & Psychological Consultation, 20*(1), 75-82. doi:10.1080/10474410903554902

Dovidio, J. F., Saguy, T., & Shnabel, N. (2009). Cooperation and conflict within groups: Bridging intragroup and intergroup processes. *Journal of Social Issues, 65*(2), 429-449.

Friend, M. (2000). Myths and misunderstandings about professional collaboration. *Remedial and Special Education, 21*(3), 130-132.

Glaser, M. A., Bruckner, M. R., & Bannon, C. (2010). Citizen attachment: Building sustainable communities. *Government Finance Review, 26*(5), 25-29.

Hudson, B. (2007). Pessimism and optimism in inter-professional working: The Sedgefield Integrated Team. *Journal of Interprofessional Care, 21*(1), 3-15.

Lasker, R. D., Weiss E. S., & Miller, R. (2001). Partnership synergy: A practical framework for studying and strengthening the collaborative advantage. *The Milbank Quarterly, 79*(2), 179-205.

Laughlin, P. R., Hatch, E. C., Silver, J. S., & Boh, L. (2006). Groups perform better than the best individuals on letters-to-numbers problems: Effects of group size. *Journal of Personality and Social Psychology, 90*(4), 644-651.

Leavitt, H., & Lipman-Blumen, J. (1995). Hot groups. *Harvard Business Review, 73*(4), 109-116.

Miller, P. M. (2008). Examining the work of boundary spanning leaders in community contexts. *International Journal of Leadership in Education, 11*(4), 353-377.

Milstein, G., Manierre, A., Susman, V. L., & Bruce, M. L. (2008). Implementation of a program to improve the continuity of mental health care through Clergy Outreach and Professional Engagement (C.O.P.E.). *Professional Psychology: Research and Practice, 39*(2), 218-228.

Mitchell, R., Parker, V., Giles, M., & White, N. (2010). Toward realizing the potential of diversity in composition of interprofessional health care teams: An examination of the cognitive and psychosocial dynamics of interprofessional collaboration. *Medical Care Research and Review, 67*(1), 3-26. doi:10.1177/1077558709338478

Morse, R. S. (2010). Integrative public leadership: Catalyzing collaboration to create public value. *The Leadership Quarterly, 21*, 231-245.

Mulvale, G., & Bourgeault, I. L. (2007). Finding the right mix: How do contextual factors affect collaborative mental health care in Ontario? *Canadian Public Policy/Analyse de Politiques, 33*, S49-S64.

Nissen, L. B. (2010). Boundary spanners revisited: A qualitative inquiry into cross-system reform through the experience of youth service professionals. *Qualitative Social Work, 9*(3), 365-384.

Notgarnie, H. M. (2011). The importance of teamwork, collaboration. *Registered Dental Hygienist, 31*(9).

O'Daniel, M., & Rosenstein, A. H. (2008). Professional communication and team collaboration. In R. G. Hughes (Ed.), *Patient safety and quality: An evidence-based handbook for nurses* (chapter 33). Rockville, MD: Agency for Healthcare Research and Quality. Retrieved from http://archive.ahrq.gov/professionals/clinicians-providers/resources/nursing/resources/nurseshdbk/nurseshdbk.pdf

Perrault, E., McClelland, R., Austin, C., & Sieppert, J. (2011). Working together in collaborations: Successful process factors for community collaboration. *Administration in Social Work, 35*(2), 282-298.

Reich, S. M., & Reich, J. A. (2006). Cultural competence in interdisciplinary collaborations: A method for respecting diversity in research partnerships. *American Journal of Community Psychology, 38,* 51-62. doi:10.1007/s10464-006-9064-1

Richter, A. W., West, M. A., van Dick, R., & Dawson, J. F. (2006). Boundary spanners' identification, intergroup contact, and effective intergroup relations. *Academy of Management Journal, 49*(6), 1252-1269.

Sawyer, R. K. (2007). *Group genius: The creative power of collaboration.* New York, NY: Basic Books.

Sawyer, R. K. (2010). Individual and group creativity. In J. C. Kaufman and R. J. Sternberg (Eds.), *The Cambridge handbook of creativity* (pp. 366–380). New York, NY: Cambridge University Press.

Sawyer, R. K. (2012). *Explaining creativity: The science of human innovation* (2nd ed.). New York, NY: Oxford University Press.

Sawyer, R. K., & DeZutter, S. (2009). Distributed creativity: How collective creations emerge from collaboration. *Psychology of Aesthetics, Creativity, and the Arts, 3*(2), 81-92.

Schwartz, D. L. (1995). The emergence of abstract representation in dyad problem solving. *Journal of the Learning Sciences 4*(3), 321-354.

Sowa, J. E. (2008). Implementing interagency collaborations: Exploring variation in collaborative ventures in human service organizations. *Administration & Society, 20*(10), 1-26.

Takahashi, L. M., & Smutny, G. (2001). Collaboration among small community-based organizations. *Journal of Planning Education and Research, 21,* 141-153.

Thompson, L. (2013). *Creative conspiracy: The new rules of breakthrough collaboration.* Boston, MA: Harvard Business Review Press.

Thomson, A. M., & Perry, J. L. (2006). Collaboration processes: Inside the black box. *Public Administration Review, 66,* 20-32.

Tuckman, B. (1965). Developmental sequence in small groups. *Psychological Bulletin, 63*(6), 384-99.

Wuchty, S., Jones, B. F., & Uzzi, B. (2007). The increasing dominance of teams in the production of knowledge. *Science, 316,* 1036-1039.

About the Author

Diane R. Bessel, PhD, LMSW, CNM, serves as Master of Social Work Program Director at Daemen College. Her research focuses on collaborative solutions to complex social problems including poverty and homelessness. She received her Master of Science in Social Administration from Case Western Reserve University and a Doctorate in Sociology from the University at Buffalo. She has also trained at the International Center for Studies in Creativity at SUNY Buffalo State, and is currently examining the use of creative problem solving within social work education.

Email: dbessel@daemen.edu
Twitter: @drbessel

How Does Creative Leadership Pave the Way for Successful Entrepreneurs?

Karina Loera Barcenas
International Center for Studies in Creativity
SUNY Buffalo State

Abstract

Entrepreneurs play a important role in the economy, creating jobs and driving much of a nation's economic activity. If entrepreneurship is defined as the successful implementation of creative ideas to produce a new business, or a new initiative within an existing business (Amabile, 1997), then entrepreneurs are by definition building and running creative enterprises. This paper argues that, as creative enterprises, entrepreneurial companies would benefit from understanding the dynamics of innovation, creativity, and creative leadership as they build their enterprises and lead their employees.

How Does Creative Leadership Pave the Way for Successful Entrepreneurs?

My father is an entrepreneur and he is my hero. I remember a crisis when we lived as a family back in 1994. My father decided to sell our home to buy a property on which he could start a new business. After years and years of seeing him waking up at 3 a.m. and traveling all the time, he finally bought a house—then three years later, he sold it. Can you imagine all the feelings that my mom, my brother and I experienced? *He sold our house!* My father was exchanging our home for a new business. We had to move and become renters again. In that moment, it seemed to be the worst possible idea. In hindsight, we could all thank my father for the decision he had made and could recognize his vision: some years later he sold that property and founded what is now his core and very successful business. I now have the opportunity to share this successful entrepreneurship story, exemplifying the importance of leading creatively while being an entrepreneur.

Entrepreneurship

Entrepreneurship can be defined as the successful implementation of creative ideas to produce a new business, or a new initiative within an existing business (Amabile, 1997). It can also be conceived of as a process by which value is created for business and social communities, by placing together unique combinations of public or private resources to exploit economic, social, or cultural opportunities in an environment of change (Fillis & Rentschler, 2010). Dino (2015) explained that entrepreneurship focuses on the identification and capture of opportunities for useful and actionable outcomes in which a need could be fulfilled, creating value; or a solution identification for an intractable problem. These entrepreneurship definitions converge on three main concepts: the identification of an opportunity or a gap; the creation of something new, unique or original; and usefulness, solving a problem or fulfilling a need.

Entrepreneurs play a core role in the economy. By developing new ventures, they create jobs, increase economic activity, and drive innovation (Ernst & Young, 2011). Baumol (2002) highlighted that job growth in the United States has been tied to entrepreneurial activity in recent years.

According to Fillis and Rentschler (2010), entrepreneurship has three underlying dimensions: innovation, risk-taking, and proactiveness. Innovation refers to a method of searching for opportunities, or the manner in which ideas are transformed into profitable and successful outcomes. Risk-taking is related to the way innovation is executed in the organization, community, or society. It also relates to the willingness of people to commit significant resources under uncertain circumstances. Proactiveness is concerned with making things happen by perseverance, adaptability, and breaking away from the established way of doing things. Proactiveness is also seen as an opportunity-seeking and forward-looking posture that involves monitoring current trends; it identifies future market demand and anticipates industrial changes or emerging opportunities (Dess & Lumpkin, 2005; Rauch, Wiklund, Lumpkin, & Frese, 2009).

The Entrepreneurial Pathway

My father, Gerardo Loera, has worked his whole life in fruit distribution and retail. He began by working for someone in *Central de Abasto*, Mexico City's public wholesale produce market. As time passed he advanced in his career by identifying needs in the fruit supply chain. His current business was born from the observation that people would not buy fruit that looked ugly and old, despite still being fresh and delicious. He realized there was a business opportunity in answering this question: *How to make people buy that ugly fruit?* He did some research and identified just one business attempting to solve this problem—and in his opinion, not very well. He gathered a team (his brothers) and resources (all their savings and properties, including our home) and founded a small business dedicated to "make up" and retail the fruit. They offered a service by which oranges, lemons, and grapefruits would be painted (with edible paint of course) and literally polished (using an organic serum) to make them not just shiny but long lasting. The serum protected the fruit from early oxidation and decomposition. That was thirteen years ago. There are now about seven companies using the same process in Mexico City, and so my father is now thinking about how to take his business to the next level.

Schumpeter (1934) explained that entrepreneurship consists of doing things that are not generally done in the ordinary course of business. Ernst & Young (2011) collected insights from 685 entrepreneurial business leaders around the world, concluding that entrepreneurs are made, not born—there is no entrepreneurship gene. Their data further showed that most entrepreneurial leaders start at a young age, and more than half transition from being an employee. Sternberg (2004) also concluded that many entrepreneurs become so because they have been dissatisfied with business environments in which they have worked.

The decision to become an entrepreneur is the first and crucial step in this process. One aspect of motivation that plays a transcendent role is "self-efficacy" (Baron, 2004). Self-efficacy can be explained as one's ability to assemble and implement necessary resources, skills, and competencies to attain a certain level of achievement on a given task (Bandura, 1997). Regarding opportunity-finding, from an effectuation perspective (i.e., entrepreneurial thinking and decision making), it can be shown that entrepreneurial opportunities are *created* rather than *observed* (McMullen & Shepherd, 2006). Creativity is potentially related to this as a direct outcome (Read & Sarasvathy, 2005); entrepreneurial decision-making may encourage one's perception and exploitation of existing individual creative skills.

What about the risk-taking? While there is literature discussing whether entrepreneurs are risk-takers at all (at least in the sense that we traditionally think about risk-taking; Ernst & Young, 2011), what is clear is that entrepreneurs challenge current states by questioning and experimenting with their own solutions, triggering change and uncertainty of outcome—which means there is a de facto risk of failure. There are three sources of risk that influence creative work (Mumford, Scott, Gaddis, & Strange, 2002): if the idea is viable; if there is assurance that the idea can be developed; and if there is assurance the idea can be successfully implemented and will serve the current market needs. French scholars Villette and Vuillermont (2009) supported the idea that successful entrepreneurs are risk minimizers who take great care to ensure that they evaluate opportunities carefully and assess the possible risk that the business might face. Fillis and Rentschler (2010) listed calculated risk taking as one of the successful entrepreneur's core characteristics.

Creativity, Innovation, and Entrepreneurship

Creativity is the production of novel and appropriate solutions to open-ended problems in any domain of human activity (Amabile, 1997); it is focused on the generation of new ideas or associations between existing concepts (Dino, 2015). *Innovation* is the implementation of those novel, appropriate ideas in some specific contexts (Amabile, 1997), with an eye toward producing outcomes that are original, useful, and actionable (Dino, 2015).

Holt (1992) defines *entrepreneurs* as those who "incubate new ideas, start enterprises based in ideas, have vision for growth, commitment to constructive change, persistence to gather necessary resources, and energy to achieve unusual results" (p. 11). *Entrepreneurship* focuses on the identification and capture of opportunities for useful and actionable outcomes in which a need could be satisfied, value created, or a solution found for an intractable problem (Dino, 2015). Entrepreneurs, as noted earlier, have the ability to identify gaps and create their own opportunities. Fillis and Rentschler (2010) found that creativity was critical all along the entrepreneurial experience, from problem identification to leadership and development of the product. This begins with the moment in which a person questions the current situation by sensing gaps or needs, then continues by finding opportunities, ideating how to satisfy those needs, searching for idea acceptance, and finally by implementing their unique solution. Fillis and Rentschler (2010) also explained that "it is the creativity of the entrepreneur that offers the best chance of stimulating business" (p. 73). Thus, the relationship between creativity, innovation and entrepreneurship is evident. In practice, creativity, innovation and entrepreneurship need each other and are equally important in a larger value-adding ecosystem (Dino, 2015).

Creative Leadership for Entrepreneurs

Mumford et al. (2002) suggested that due to the strong relationship and commonalities between the creative person and the creative work, a model for the leadership of creative ventures should be built. Tushman and O'Reilly (1997) emphasized that creative leadership needs to be studied because effective leadership makes innovation possible, and thus organizational adaptation and growth are possible. But, why is the leadership of creative ventures unique? Different leadership styles may significantly influence creative work (Runco, 2014). Mumford et al. (2002) noted that since creative efforts present novel and ill-defined tasks, the leaders cannot just rely on predefined structures but, instead, must be capable of creating a structure and providing direction to work where there is no inherent direction. Fillis & Rentschler (2010) stated that creative leadership is often deemed more appropriate than conventional managerial methods in the quest to deal with non-linear and often unpredictable conditions. Additionally, Sawyer (2012) claimed that creative leaders have differentiated impact because they can motivate their teams in more effective ways, and are particularly good at handling novel challenges that force them to break with typical routines. Puccio, Mance, and Murdock (2011) defined *creative leadership* as:

> the ability to deliberately engage ones' imagination to define and guide a group towards a novel goal—a direction that is new for the group. As a consequence of bringing about this creative change, creative leaders have a profoundly positive influence on their context and the individuals in that situation. (p. 13)

This definition mirrors the characteristics that an entrepreneur should practice as a leader while pursuing a venture's success. Hence, it seems natural that entrepreneurs should practice creative leadership to drive creative change that leads to innovation.

The Creative Change Model: A Systems Approach Framing Entrepreneurs' Creative Leadership Operation

In trying to understand how creativity operates, Rhodes (1961) described four elements, commonly known as the 4 Ps: person, process, product, and press (sometimes simplified as meaning the environment in which creativity happens, but also including the various elements that press upon creative action). Since then, Rhodes' construct has had some thoughtful additions. Simonton (1990) added a fifth P, persuasion, based on the evidence that creators often need to advocate for and persuade others to accept their creations. Puccio et al. (2011) placed Rhodes' construct into a system using the main four elements plus leadership as the "lubricant" that allows the four elements to interact effectively—or not.

We can now examine person, process, press, product, and persuasion in the context of creative leadership.

The *person(s)* element considers individual elements such as skills, knowledge, personality, experiences, and motivation, all of which influence the type and amount of creativity a person (or a group of persons) is likely to produce (Puccio, et al., 2011). Mumford et al. (2002) explained that the creative leader should be the technical expert, that he or she should be capable of triggering intellectual stimulation or the application of creative problem-solving techniques in guiding others; he or she also should be able to provide guidance, and set clear expectations while identifying and integrating the goals.

A particular behavior of entrepreneurial persons is effectuation. Dew, Read, Sarasvathy, and Wiltbank (2009), and Sarasvathy (2001), described *effectuation* as a particular entrepreneurial decision-making logic that relies on control rather than on prediction, and it is based on four conditions: *starting point of venturing,* focusing on available means instead of using a goal orientation; *attitude towards risk,* investing what one can afford to lose rather than trying to forecast expected returns; *approach towards stakeholders,* relying on partnerships instead of competitive analysis; and *association with contingencies,* embracing unexpected events rather than avoiding them. Effectuators approach decision making by embracing the ambiguity inherent in it, and by learning how to consider the possibility of failure in their plans.

From another perspective, Sternberg (1997) described *successful intelligence* as the ability to achieve what one seeks in life, within one's sociocultural context, through a combination of adapting, shaping, and selecting environments, and with a mix of analytical, creative, and practical abilities. He suggested that successful intelligence could be a basis for entrepreneurs: one needs creative intelligence to come up with new ideas; analytical intelligence to evaluate whether the ideas are good ones; and practical intelligence to figure out a way to sell those ideas to people who may not want to hear about them. He emphasized that each of the three are equally important for successful entrepreneurship.

Process refers to the stages that individuals or groups traverse as they develop creative ideas in response to opportunities (Puccio et al., 2011). Creative Problem Solving (CPS) is a comprehensive cognitive and affective system built on our natural creative processes that deliberately ignites creative thinking and, as a result, generates creative solutions and changes (Puccio, et al., 2011). Findings demonstrate that creative problem solving skills in a leader directly influence the creative outcome of followers (Mumford et al., 2002). It is easily seen that CPS can greatly contribute to the entrepreneurial practice, due to the entrepreneur's constant need to address challenges while facing uncertainty. CPS is a map that entrepreneurs can follow to design their structures and strategies. By learning and practicing CPS, leaders can boost and better direct their thinking as it is applied to situations that require novel solutions (Puccio et al., 2011).

The *press* (or *environment*) refers to the ways in which the psychological and physical workplace climate and culture impacts and influences the expression of creative behavior (Puccio et al., 2011). Different social influences and settings have different results in different people (Runco, 2014). The design of the environment can trigger certain behaviors. Findings support the idea that leaders must pay attention to the details of their *own everyday behaviors* toward subordinates (Amabile, Schatzel, Moneta, & Kramer, 2004). Entrepreneurs as leaders must also be diligent observers of their followers. Mumford et al. (2002) noted that leaders must ensure diversity in the group; permit open communications; and, through role modeling, crisis management, and policy decisions, seek to create a climate and culture where people are likely to look for innovative ideas. Amabile (1990) presented a model with eight measurable climate dimensions: organizational encouragement, encouragement by supervisors, freedom within the organization, pressure and workload, resources, organizational hurdles and impediments, challenging work and assignments, and support for work groups. Entrepreneurs should pay attention and identify how to modify the environment's dimensions to engage their teams and inspire creative action and project engagement. The "press" element, then, is not just about the physical environment, but getting to know what motivates the employees and how to include those considerations while communicating with them. Amabile (1997) suggested that entrepreneurs should consider synergistic extrinsic motivators while molding an idea to be appropriate for the market. Attention to the outside world is necessary to gather information that will contribute to commercial success. A dynamic between intrinsic and synergistic extrinsic motivators is needed while managing a group through all venture stages.

Product. The interaction of the entrepreneur (the creative person) following a certain process in an environment that might change, but that also can be adapted, results in a product. This product is the solution that represents the innovation outcome. It can be tangible or intangible, containing novelty and usefulness within (Puccio, et al., 2011). Rhodes (1961) defined the product as something novel and appropriate by the relevant social group. Sawyer (2012) explained creativity through a sociocultural definition: "Creativity is the generation of a product that is judged to be novel and also to be appropriate, useful or valuable by a suitably knowledgeable social group" (p. 8). When this venture is successful it becomes innovation. Entrepreneurship is then a particular form of innovation (Amabile, 1997).

Persuasion means that creative people change the way other people think (Runco, 2014; Simonton, 1990). In their integrative system for creative leadership, Mumford et al. (2002) presented the concept of "idea promotion," which involves gathering support from the broader organization for the creative enterprise as a whole, as well as for implementation of a specific idea or project (p. 739). The Ernst and Young (2011) report brought out a different but still interesting perspective of persuasion: they found that traditional companies can learn from entrepreneurial leaders. This supports the idea that entrepreneurship impact goes beyond changing ways of thinking, but also helps create new ways of running business.

The entrepreneur plays the role of a creative leader when he or she as a person sets the creative environment for followers to engage in the creative process. If the creative venture adds value to an individual, team, organization, or society, creative change happens.

Conclusion and Final Thoughts

My father didn't know that creativity and its elements played an important role in his entrepreneurial work execution, yet he is running a venture that is adding value in the market. He is always preparing himself, reading and being aware of what is happening. He treats his employees as family, but still is quite objective, clear and fair. When he faces a problem, he gathers his team and together they find a solution. He and his collaborators are always seeking better ways to optimize the business, to identify potential clients, and to improve their service. I would say that he loves his job, and that there are two main things that motivate him: the sensation of accomplishment, and all the fruits that his venture means to his family. I have witnessed that he is continuously adapting himself, his resources, and his expectations. I wonder what would have happened if my father knew all the ways in which he can boost his creative leadership while running his venture, beyond what he does naturally. Entrepreneurs are filled with passion and a need for taking risks while solving problems or filling gaps. They know there is no parachute and still they continue forward. Facing an uncertain and sometimes wild environment, they adapt and evolve towards their dynamic—constantly changing—goals. Entrepreneurs are creative whether they realize it or not. Wouldn't it be great to invite them to learn how to more deliberately be creative, and more effectively be a creative leader?

References

Amabile, T. M. (1990). Within you, without you: Towards a social psychology of creativity, and beyond. In M. A. Runco & R. S. Albert (Eds.), *Theories of creativity* (pp. 61-91). Newbury Park, CA: Sage Publications.

Amabile, T. M. (1997). Entrepreneurial creativity through motivational synergy. *Journal of Creative Behavior, 31*(1), 18-26.

Amabile, T. M., Schatzel, E. A., Moneta, G. B., & Kramer, S. J. (2004). Leader behaviors and the work environment for creativity: Perceived leader support. *The Leadership Quarterly, 15,* 5-32.

Bandura, A. (1997). *Self-efficacy: The exercise of control.* New York, NY: Freeman.

Baron, R. A. (2004). The cognitive perspective: A valuable tool for answering entrepreneurship's basic "why" questions. *Journal of Business Venturing, 19,* 221-239. doi: 10.1016/S0883-9026(03)00008-9.

Baumol, W. J. (2002). *The free-market innovation machine: Analyzing the growth miracle of capitalism.* Princeton, NJ: Princeton University Press.

Dess, G. G., & Lumpkin, G. T. (2005). The role of entrepreneurial orientation in stimulating effective corporate entrepreneurship. *Academy of Management Executive, 19,* 147-56.

Dew, N., Read, S., Sarasvathy, S., & Wiltbank, R. (2009). Effectual versus predictive logics in entrepreneurial decision making: Differences between experts and novices. *Journal of Business Venturing, 24,* 287-309.

Dino, R. N. (2015). Crossing boundaries: Toward integrating creativity, innovation, and entrepreneurship research through practice. *Psychology of Aesthetics, Creativity and the Arts, 9*(2), 139-146.

Ernst & Young (2011). *Nature or nurture: Decoding the DNA of the entrepreneur.* Retrieved from http://www.entrepreneurship.org/resource-center/~/media/Entrepreneurship/Files/Resource%20Center/Nature_or_nurture_FINAL.pdf

Fillis, I., & Rentschler, R. (2010). The role of creativity in entrepreneurship. *Journal of Enterprising Culture, 18*(1), 49-81. doi: 10.1142/S0218495810000501

Holt, D. H. (1992). *Entrepreneurship: New venture creation*. Englewood Cliffs, NJ: Prentice-Hall.

Mumford, M. D., Scott, G. M., Gaddis, B., & Strange, J. M. (2002). Leading creative people: Orchestrating expertise and relationships. *The Leadership Quarterly, 13,* 705-750.

Puccio, G. J., Mance, M., & Murdock, M. C. (2011). *Creative leadership: Skills that drive change* (2nd ed.). Thousand Oaks, CA: Sage Publications.

Rauch, A., Wiklund, J., Lumpkin, G. T., & Frese, M. (2009). Entrepreneurial orientation and business performance: An assessment of past research and suggestions for the future. *Entrepreneurship: Theory and Practice, 33,* 761-787.

Read, S., & Sarasvathy, S. (2005). Knowing what to do and doing what you know: Effectuation as a form of entrepreneurial expertise. *Journal of Private Equity, 9,* 45-62.

Rhodes, M. (1961). An analysis of creativity. *Phi Delta Kappan, 42*(7), 305-310.

Runco, M. A. (2014). *Creativity: Theories and themes: Research, development and practice* (2nd ed.). San Diego, CA: Academic Press.

Sarasvathy, S. (2001) Causation and effectuation: Toward a theoretical shift from economic inevitability to entrepreneurial contingency. *Academy of Management Review, 26,* 243-263.

Sawyer, R. K. (2012). *Explaining creativity: The science of human innovation* (2nd ed.). New York, NY: Oxford University Press.

Schumpeter, J. A. (1934). *The theory of economical development*. Cambridge, MA: Harvard University Press.

Simonton, D. K. (1990). History, chemistry, psychology, and genius: An intellectual autobiography of histometry. In M. A. Runco & R. S. Albert (Eds.), *Theories of creativity* (pp. 61-91). Newbury Park, CA: Sage Publications.

Sternberg, R. J. (1997). *Successful intelligence*. New York, NY: Plume.

Sternberg, R. J. (2004). Successful intelligence as a basis for entrepreneurship. *Journal of Business Venturing, 19,* 189-201.

Tushman, M. L., & O'Reilly, C. A. (1997). *Winning through innovation*. Cambridge, MA: Harvard Business Review Press.

Villette, M., & Vuillermot, C. (2009). *From predators to icons: Exposing the myth of the business*. Ithaca, NY: ILR Press.

About the Author

Karina Loera Barcenas has a Marketing B.A. from Instituto Tecnológico y de Estudios Superiores de Monterrey (ITESM), Ciudad de Mexico. She worked at Eli Lilly Mexico for almost eight years in different positions such as sales strategy specialist, Keflex brand manager and Cialis product manager. She has an M.S. in Creativity from SUNY Buffalo State, where she received the Mary Murdock award in 2015. She has been working with entrepreneurs at the Small Business Development Center at Buffalo State and also managing the Buffalo State Business Incubator. Karina is currently a coach in Centro de Certificacion en Creatividad. At the International Center for Studies in Creativity, she is conducting research with Dr. Selcuk Acar and is an adjunct instructor for undergraduate courses. Karina is part of the core team of the CPSI conference. She is a fixer by nature and a creativity preacher by heart. Her current area of interest is the world of entrepreneurship, leadership, and creativity.

Email: kaloba@gmail.com
LinkedIn: www.linkedin.com/in/karina-loera-30814535

PERSONAL CREATIVITY

How Can Parents Fan the Spark of Their Children's Creativity?

Lina Pugsley
International Center for Studies in Creativity
SUNY Buffalo State

Abstract

Ken Robinson (2012) brought much attention to the significance of creativity in the educational system in his TED Talk "Do Schools Kill Creativity?"—but what about *parents?* What role do parents play in cultivating capacities for creativity in children? This paper explores the critical role that parents play in establishing a strong foundation for developing creativity in children from birth to age six. The parent-child relationship is examined with a focus on identifying key social conditions that inspire and nurture creativity. Conditions for fostering creativity include establishing a home environment where respect is prioritized; promoting independence and decision making; modeling and encouraging an attitude for creativity; and providing a nurturing and affirming creative climate.

How Can Parents Fan the Spark of Their Children's Creativity?

Fan the Spark

Your children plan their own education,
like it or not.
You must learn to cooperate with that plan.
If they are drawing,
they become artists.
If they are reading,
they become students.
If they are investigating something,
they become scientists.
If they are helping prepare a meal,
they become chefs.
Whatever they are doing, they are learning.
And it is, for them,
pure joy.

Can you refrain from judging their interests?
Can you give them room to explore?
Schools do not often do this.
You may be the only one
who can fan the spark of their creativity
into a flame of joy.

— William Martin (1999, p. 48)

In the decade since Ken Robinson (2006) gave his now-legendary TED Talk "Do Schools Kill Creativity?", educational systems around the world have been under scrutiny for not actively promoting creativity in classrooms (Anderson, 2015). Robinson (2012) has continued to bring awareness to the fact that we are all "born with deep natural capacities for creativity and systems of mass education tend to suppress them" (para. 4). Robinson highlighted the increasingly urgent need to cultivate capacities for creativity and to rethink the dominant approaches to education. But what about parents? As I watched this talk for the first time, around the time my first child was born, I started thinking about ways I could make sure that I, as a parent, don't kill creativity in my child.

Rather than relying on the school system and hoping for educational reform in time for when my child would arrive there in just a few short years, I decided I needed to understand *how* to support and cultivate my children's capacities for creativity. The more I thought about it, the more I was convinced that the interactions parents have with their babies and children in the early years establish the foundations for creative development and creativity realized later in life (Millar, 2002). I decided that rather than wait for schools to nurture and encourage my children's creativity, I would do it myself, for each of my children starting at birth.

To begin, I made it my mission to understand the issue: the conditions necessary for creative development in children, the parent-child relational aspects of cultivating creativity, and how to establish environments where creativity can flourish. I quickly found that little research exists on how the foundation of creativity can and should be instilled in children in the early years (Domino, 1969; Mindham, 2005; Tennent & Berthelsen, 1997). In a time where the value of creativity is so high—Brown (2010) wrote that "the only unique contribution that we will ever make in this world will be born of our creativity" (p. 96)—it perplexes me to think that little work has been done to examine *how* to establish positive creative habits from the very start of life.

This paper will explore the critical role of the parent in establishing conditions for creative growth in the early years of childhood, from birth to age six. Three factors that influence creativity in the family context will be examined through a mindful parenting lens: parental attitudes toward creativity; relational aspects of parent-child interactions; and creativity-fostering environments, both psychological climate and physical space.

What is Mindfulness?

Mindfulness is the "awareness that emerges through paying attention on purpose, in the present moment, and non-judgmentally to the unfolding of experiences moment by moment" (Kabat-Zinn, 2003, p. 145). It is maintaining awareness in the present moment of our thoughts, feelings, bodily sensations, and surrounding environments, and at the same time recognizing our thoughts and feelings without judging them as good or bad, or believing that there is a "right" or "wrong" way to think or feel in a given moment. Qualities associated with mindfulness are acceptance, non-judgment, curiosity, and observation. Studies show that practicing mindfulness enhances relationships (Carson, Carson, Gil, & Baucom, 2004), and report that mindful parents are happier with their parenting skills and their relationships with their kids (Carter, 2009). Bringing mindfulness into parenting and family life is an application of mindfulness that appears to be growing in appeal to parents.

What is Mindful Parenting?

Parenting mindfully means providing children with the precious gift of full presence and being in the moment. It is deliberately and intentionally bringing "purposeful awareness to everyday parenting situations to address the deeper needs of children in order to cultivate and deepen the parent-child connection" (Placone, n. d.). Although empirical evidence is still sparse, mindful parenting programs and groups are gaining momentum, particularly in the field of behavioral health (Bögels & Restifo, 2013). Broad conceptualization of how daily practices of mindfulness are readily applicable to parenting and the parent-child relationship have been developed through a five dimensional model: (a) listening with full attention; (b) nonjudgmental acceptance of self and child; (c) emotional awareness of self and child; (d) self-regulation in the parenting relationship; and (e) compassion for self and child (Duncan, Coatsworth, & Greenberg, 2009). The suggested benefits of mindful parenting based on this model include, but are not limited to, improved quality of parent-child relationships and the ability to bring a present-moment awareness to parenting. This includes listening with full attention and bringing emotional awareness and nonjudgmental acceptance to parenting interactions.

Mindful Parenting and Parental Attitudes Toward Creativity

A good place to begin in examining parental attitudes toward creativity and the impact of parents' attitudes on creative development in children, is to ask the questions: Do parents value creativity? Is the answer to this question a determining factor of creative learning in the child? Torrance (1965) postulated if children are to develop creativity then parents must value those personality characteristics that will ensure the development of their children's creative potentials. In an effort to understand parental attitudes toward children's characteristics, Torrance (1975) developed the Ideal Child Checklist. This 66-item true/false question list evaluates what kind of person parents would like their children to become and identifies desirable and undesirable characteristics as viewed by parents. Checklist items included, for example, "adventurous, testing limits," "conforming," "emotionally sensitive," and "spirited in disagreement." Torrance found that certain characteristics such as stubbornness, independent thinking, risk taking, nonconformity, and sensitivity characterized the creative individual, yet are qualities that were easily discouraged when misunderstood. The results serve as a means for teachers and parents to be mindful of conditions necessary for the nurturance of creative potential.

Parenting Style and Creativity

Developmental psychologists have long been interested in understanding how parents impact child development (Cherry, 2014). Researchers have studied cause-and-effect links between specific actions of parents and later behavior of children to determine links between parenting styles and child behaviors.

The seminal work of Baumrind (1966) and Maccoby and Martin (1983) identified four styles of parenting: authoritative, authoritarian, permissive, and neglectful.

> An *authoritative* style exhibits high levels of responsiveness and demand-ingness. Authoritative parents make reasonable demands, but are very accepting of their children as well. An *authoritarian* style exhibits a high level of demandingness but a low level of responsiveness. Authoritarian parents are very strict with their children and emphasize discipline over nurturing. A *permissive* style exhibits a low level of demandingness but a high level of responsiveness. Permissive parents are very accepting but exhibit less control over their children. (Miller, Lambert, & Speirs, 2012, p. 346; italics added)

Neglectful or indifferent parents are generally uninvolved, and therefore make few demands, exercise little control, show little affection, and do not communicate often (Maccoby & Martin, 1983).

Dacey and Packer (1992) defined a parenting style that, unlike authoritative parenting, provides children with more autonomy and the opportunities to set their own priorities based on intrinsically-motivated goals. Based on a four-year study of highly creative children, they identified the *nurturing parent* style:

> Nurturing parents respect their children's autonomy, thoughts, and feelings. Rather than imposing priorities, they encourage children to find their own. They do not pressure, they support...they provide their children with a clear structure of values that encourages self-discipline, commitment, and intellectual and creative freedom. (Dacey & Packer, 1992, p. 38)

The motivation behind this study was the researchers' belief that "most of a child's personality is learned, and that the most powerful force acting upon that personality is the parents' style of child-raising" (Dacey & Packer, 1992, p. 13). The nurturing parent style is based on six fundamental principles: trust, respect, support, enjoyment, protection, and role modeling. A significant aspect of the nurturing parent approach is practicing mindfulness in an effort to raise creative, loving, responsible children who grow up to be creative, loving, and responsible adults who are in tune with who they are (Dacey & Packer, 1992).

The Relationship Between Parenting Style and Creativity

Does parenting style actually impact children's creativity? The research suggests that it does (Fearon, Copeland, & Saxon, 2013; Harrington, Block, & Block, 1987; Miller et al., 2012; Tennent & Berthelsen, 1997). Studies have shown that both authoritative and permissive parenting styles are associated with higher levels of creativity in children (Miller et al., 2012). Parents of highly creative children exhibited greater expressiveness with lesser dominance and were seen as exhibiting extraordinary respect for their children and confidence in their abilities. Additional findings revealed that mothers of creative children exhibit greater self-assurance, initiative, and interpersonal competence; they prefer change and unstructured demands; they are more insightful about others, are more tolerant, and value autonomy and independent endeavors (Domino, 1969).

Researchers have questioned what parenting qualities trigger negative creative outcomes in children. Specific characteristics of the authoritarian style that negatively affect creativity have not been defined (Miller et al., 2012). However, the literature has indicated that responsiveness, "the use of warm and accepting behaviors to respond to children's needs and signals" (Landry et al., 2012), a condition present in permissive and authoritative styles, had positive relationships with creativity—which also explains why the authoritarian parenting style, low in responsiveness, was usually negatively related to creativity (Miller et al., 2012). Authoritarian mothers are less likely to provide home environments conducive to creativity, due to restrictive environments that inhibit growing independence, the physical means of discipline, and the expectation that children not make mistakes (Tennant & Berthelsen, 1997).

Given what the research has uncovered, how does one explain neglected children who are highly creative? Again, little documented research exists to explain the specific factors involved, however Amabile (1989) found intriguing research evidence that suggests upsets, traumas, and tragedies in a child's life will not necessarily undermine creativity but may even enhance it. One study showed "that highly creative children actually suffered a greater number of traumas than ordinary children" (Amabile, 1989, p. 123). In addition, a longitudinal study showed a positive relationship between parental conflict and later adult creativity (Koestner, Walker, & Fichman, 1999).

The consensus among almost all studies that discuss parenting style in relation to creativity is that "creative children appear to have parents who treat them with respect, have confidence in their abilities, give them responsibility with autonomy and freedom, and expect them to do well" (Miller & Gerard, 1979).

Parent-Child Relationship and the Climate for Creativity

Interactions between parent and child, beginning from infancy and continuing through toddlerhood and preschool years, are the initial opportunities for the development of creativity in young children. Parents and early childhood educators tend to focus on fostering children's development in the cognitive, emotional, social, physical, and language domains, yet promoting the development of creativity is a domain that is less often, or at least less explicitly, stated (Kemple & Nissenberg, 2000).

Opportunities to enhance creativity in young children through relational aspects can be found in the arenas of respect, independence, encouraging creative thinking, play, establishing a psychological climate for creativity, and establishing a creative climate in the home. We will cover each of these in turn.

Respect the Child

"If only people would trust nature's plan for how babies are created, they could relax and enjoy all the daily miracles of natural development" (Gerber, 2002, p. 11). The first and arguably the most important basis of cultivating creativity is to respect and trust a healthy, normal baby's inborn capabilities, and his natural desire to learn (Gerber, 2002). Providing infants with the opportunities and time to take in and figure out the world around them is the basis of a mindful parenting philosophy for infant care developed by Magda Gerber, through the organization she founded called Resources for Infant Educarers (RIE). RIE is based on the work of Dr. Emmi Pickler, a Hungarian pediatrician, who introduced new theories of infant education based on respecting the child's natural development, and allowing each child to develop without interference at his or her own rate (Gerber, 2002). By respecting a child's innate abilities, parents provide the gift of promoting self-confidence, body awareness, social attentiveness, and responsiveness (Gerber, 2002).

An example of relational respect between parent and child is the non-interference with infants' internal drives to accomplish mastery of tasks. Parents' respect of, for example, their infant practicing the same activity in seemingly endless repetition, provides the child space to explore and develop at his or her own pace. By not teaching and stimulating infants at each stage of development, and instead respecting infants' developmental needs, we allow them to solve their own problems and we provide an environment in which they can experience, discover, and create (Gerber, 2002). It is up to parents to intentionally establish this type of respectful relationship for nurturing creativity.

Promote Independence

"A common key component of the house in which a creative individual was reared, is that children were allowed to become independent" (Carlson, 2008, p. 13). Creating an environment for independence means providing time and space for creative thinking. In turn, by offering both the freedom and the psychological safety to explore, experiment, and make decisions, children are encouraged to take risks with new and unfamiliar ideas (Kemple & Nissenberg, 2000). Important to recognize is that a child who feels secure in his or her relationship with the primary caregivers will be more apt to take risks and experiment with independence (Carlson, 2008).

Encourage Creative Thinking

"Homes that nurture creative children are homes where both adults and children have 'creative habits'" (Amabile, 1989, p. 120). Amabile suggested that one can make creativity a habit by consistently asking questions such as: "How can we do this differently?", "What else?", and "What if…?" In order to promote creativity, parents should engage children to investigate and explore their curiosities through questioning assumptions, discussions, debates, and experimenting together (Amabile, 1989).

Play

"Research has shown a direct connection between playfulness and creativity: children who have spent time playing tend to be more creative on tasks they do immediately afterward than children who go directly from one task to another" (Amabile, 1989). The caution for parents in playing with their children is to ensure they avoid over-controlling and correcting how the child plays (Gerber, 2002).

Creative-Fostering Environments

Next to awareness of attitude toward creativity, I believe that establishing a psychological climate for creativity is the most unrecognized opportunity parents have to cultivate capacities for creativity in their children. It is arguably the most difficult to implement as it requires a high level of attunement to recognize instances when psychological conditions are present and when they are lacking. Based on Rogers's (1954) theory of creative environments, creativity is most apt to occur when three internal psychological conditions are present: *openness to experience, an internal locus of evaluation,* and *the ability to toy with elements and concepts.* Rogers suggested that these three internal conditions are fostered by the establishment of two external conditions: *psychological safety* and *psychological freedom.* This theory aligns well with the philosophy and psychology of mindful parenting. Unconditional love, full acceptance, and being heard and listened to are examples of a psychologically safe climate characterized by unconditional worth. Additional external environmental factors for establishing a psychologically safe climate include the absence of external evaluation, and empathetic understanding of individuals (Harrington et al., 1987). Psychological freedom is established when an individual feels free to explore and create. "Rogers's theory of creativity suggests that children raised by parents who provide conditions of psychological safety and freedom will develop their creative potential more fully than will children whose parents do not provide such conditions" (Harrington et al., 1987, p. 855).

Amabile (1989) devised an assessment called "A Test for Creative Childhood Environments" to help parents determine how well their home environment is supporting their children's intrinsic motivation and creativity. This 50-item true-or-false list engages parents in thinking about aspects of creative environments, such as: "I can ask questions here at home without worrying about sounding dumb," "There are a lot of rules here at home," "My parents use bribes to get me to do what they want," or "My parents respect me." Key themes include: assessment, respect, non-judgment, curiosity, praise and reward, and freedom and autonomy. As a self-reporting measure, responses can be checked against an answer key that indicates which answers are representative of a creativity-supporting environment.

Establish a Physical Environment for Creativity in the Home

Designing physical spaces where creativity can flourish is a deliberate practice that takes some thought and planning. What might be all the ways to design physical creative spaces in the home?

Create a creativity station or "yes space." A creativity station is a place where children can explore projects and tinker with the materials available (see Figure 1). Children can take the lead and construct their own learning by using the various materials provided (Gandini, 2011). A similar idea is a "yes space," a safe place in the home where children seldom (or ever) are told "no," where they can explore the materials independently, in whatever manner they wish (see Figure 2). Mindful parenting groups such as RIE encourage "yes spaces" as they provide opportunities for babies and toddlers to play independently for extended periods of time. This is a child's opportunity to investigate her curiosities, practice developmental skills, explore, play, daydream, or anything she chooses. By supporting a child's unique way of trying things out, parents "foster an experimental attitude toward the world" (Squires, 1989, p. 12).

Figure 1: A Creativity Station. Source: L. Pugsley, used with permission.

Figure 2: A "Yes Space." Source: B. K. Hoover, used with permission.

Conclusion

What drives my passion for nurturing creativity in the early years—and beyond? It is my vision of all the wonderful qualities I'd like my children to possess, such as independence, confidence, passion, and personal fulfillment. I believe respecting children and establishing a supportive and nurturing climate is essential for helping children reach their fullest potentials and achieve whatever it is they dream to achieve. I believe that parenting mindfully, with a "nurturing parent" style, builds children who are creative thinkers, and as such are able to tune into their internal loci of evaluation, which act as their guides or compasses in life, in the quest for reaching their full potentials, and—I'll even go a step further—their purposes in life.

Parents play a critical role in establishing how children learn to relate to the world and how they see themselves in it, often without intentionally setting out to do so. Further research is needed on the relationship between mindful parenting and developing creative potential, and on how parents can deliberately nurture creativity through mindfulness of their interactions with their children. Further discussion is needed about how to raise awareness of parenting's direct effect on our children's creative potential, keeping in mind that even small changes can make a big difference.

References

Amabile, T. M. (1989). *Growing up creative: Nurturing a lifetime of creativity.* Buffalo, NY: Creative Education Foundation.

Anderson, J. (2015, December 1). *The case for restoring creativity in our schools.* Retrieved from http://qz.com/561804/the-case-for-restoring-creativity-in-our-schools

Baumrind, D. (1966). Effects of authoritative parental control on child behavior. *Child Development, 37*(4), 887-907.

Bögels, S., & Restifo, K. (2013). *Mindful parenting: A guide for mental health practitioners.* New York, NY: Springer.

Brown, B. (2010). *The gifts of imperfection: Let go of who you think you're supposed to be and embrace who you are.* Center City, MN: Hazelden.

Carlson, G. (2008). *Child of wonder: Nurturing creative and naturally curious children.* Eugene, OR: Common Ground Press.

Carson, J. W., Carson, K. M., Gil, K. M., & Baucom, D. H. (2004). Mindfulness-based relationship enhancement. *Behavior Therapy, 35,* 471-494.

Carter, C. (2009, September 2). *Losing my mindfulness*. Retrieved from http://greatergood.berkeley.edu/raising_happiness/post/losing_my_mindfulness

Cherry, K. (2014, October 12). *The 4 styles of parenting*. Retrieved from http://psychology.about.com/od/developmentalpsychology/a/parenting-style.htm

Dacey, J. S., & Packer, A. J. (1992). *The nurturing parent: How to raise creative, loving, responsible children*. New York, NY: Simon & Schuster.

Domino, G. (1969). Maternal personality correlates of sons' creativity. *Journal of Consulting and Clinical Psychology, 33*(2), 180-183.

Duncan, L. G., Coatsworth, J. D., & Greenberg, M. T. (2009). A model of mindful parenting: Implications for parent–child relationships and prevention research. *Clinical Child and Family Psychology Review, 12*(3), 255-270.

Fearon, D. D., Copeland, D., & Saxon, T. F. (2013). The relationship between parenting styles and creativity in a sample of Jamaican children. *Creativity Research Journal, 25*(1), 119-128.

Gandini, L. (2011). Play and the hundred languages of children. *American Journal of Play, 4*(1), 1-18.

Gerber, M. (2002). *Dear parent: Caring for infants with respect*. Los Angeles, CA: Resources for Infant Educarers (RIE).

Harrington, D. M., Block, J. H., & Block, J. (1987). Testing aspects of Carl Rogers' theory of creative environments: Child-rearing antecedents of creative potential in young adolescents. *Journal of Personality and Social Psychology, 52*(4), 851-856.

Kabat-Zinn, J. (2003). Mindfulness-based interventions in context: Past, present, and future. *Clinical Psychology: Science and Practice, 10*(2), 144-156.

Kemple, K. M., & Nissenberg, S. A. (2000). Nurturing creativity in early childhood education: Families are part of it. *Early Childhood Education Journal, 28*(1), 67-71.

Koestner, R., Walker, M., & Fichman, L. (1999). Childhood parenting experiences and adult creativity. *Journal of Research in Personality, 33*, 92-107.

Landry, S. H., Smith, K. E., Swank, P. R., Zucker, T., Crawford, A. D., & Solari, E. F. (2012). The effects of a responsive parenting intervention on parent-child interactions during shared book reading. *Developmental Psychology, 48*(4), 969-986.

Maccoby, E. E., & Martin, J. A. (1983). Socialization in the context of the family: Parent-child interaction. *Handbook of Child Psychology, 4*, 1-102.

Martin, W. (1999). *The parent's Tao Te Ching: A new interpretation: Ancient advice for modern parents.* New York, NY: Marlowe.

Millar, G. (2002). *The Torrance kids at mid-life: Selected case studies of creative behavior.* Westport, CT: Ablex Publishing.

Miller, A. L., Lambert, A. D., & Speirs, N. K. L. (2012). Parenting style, perfectionism, and creativity in high-ability and high-achieving young adults. *Journal for the Education of the Gifted, 35*(4), 344-365.

Miller, B. C., & Gerard, D. (1979). Family influences on the development of creativity in children: An integrative review. *Family Coordinator, 28*(3), 295-312.

Mindham, C. (2005). Creativity and the young child. *Early Years: An International Journal of Research and Development, 25*(1), 81-84.

Placone, P. M. (n.d.). *Mindful parent happy child.* Retrieved from http://www.mindfulparenthappychild.com

Robinson, K. (2006). *Do schools kill creativity?* [Video file.] Retrieved from http://www.ted.com/talks/ken_robinson_says_schools_kill_creativity

Robinson, K. (2012, December 7). *Do schools kill creativity?* Retrieved from http://www.huffingtonpost.com/sir-ken-robinson/do-schools-kill-creativity_b_2252942.html

Rogers, C. R. (1954). Toward a theory of creativity. *ETC: A Review of General Semantics, 11*(4), 249-260.

Squires, S. (1989, January 17). *Creativity: Where it all begins: Letting your child be as inventive as Shakespeare...Rodin...Einstein.* Retrieved from https://www.highbeam.com/doc/1P2-1169537.html

Tennent, L., & Berthelsen, D. (1997). Creativity: What does it mean in the family context? *Journal of Australian Research in Early Childhood Education, 1,* 91-104.

Torrance, E. P. (1965). *Rewarding creative behavior.* Englewood Cliffs, NJ: Prentice Hall.

Torrance, E. P. (1975). *Preliminary manual: Ideal child checklist.* Athens, GA: Georgia Studies of Creative Behavior.

About the Author

Lina Pugsley is a creativity expert, consultant, and researcher passionate about raising global awareness of the opportunity adults face to cultivate capacities for creativity in children, so that they might build creative confidence, resilience, and innovative thinking skills. As a speaker, writer, and founder of Keeping Creativity Alive, an online resource that helps parents and teachers to promote creativity at home as well as in schools, she inspires parents to shift perspectives, defer judgment, and model living a creative life. Lina holds an M.S. in Creativity from the International Center for Studies in Creativity at SUNY Buffalo State. Her current research investigates the relationship between parenting styles and attitudes and values towards creativity in young children.

Website: keepingcreativityalive.com
Facebook: facebook.com/keepingcreativityalive
Twitter: @creativityalive

Why is Creativity in the Self-help Section? The Intersection of Creativity and Positive Psychology

Molly Holinger
International Center for Studies in Creativity
SUNY Buffalo State

Abstract

This paper explores the overlap in theory and application of positive psychology and creativity research. Martin Seligman's (2012) PERMA model of well-being provides the framework for comparison: How do creativity and positive psychology approach positive emotion, engagement, positive relationships, meaning, and accomplishment or achievement? Finally, this essay suggests further applications of creativity and positive psychology research to mutually enhance creativity and well-being.

Why is Creativity in the Self-help Section? The Intersection of Creativity and Positive Psychology

For anyone searching for a creativity book in Barnes and Noble, here is some time-saving advice: skip the psychology section, bypass the business section, and head straight for self-help. A goldmine of creativity books sits between titles like *Your Best Life Begins Each Morning* (Osteen, 2008) and *The Power of Now* (Tolle, 1999).

This forms the starting point for a question: Why are creativity books shelved there, and not generally with the fields of psychology or education that provided the basis for much of the creativity research in the last 60 years?

As the booksellers at Barnes and Noble apparently recognize, while creativity has long been associated with mental illness, so too has it been associated with mental health. Maslow (1971) believed, "The concept of creativeness and the concept of the healthy, self-actualizing, fully human person seem to be coming closer and closer together, and may turn out to be the same thing" (p. 57). According to extensive research (Davis, 2004), the creative person tends to be high energy, curious, open minded, and tolerant of ambiguity. Those who practice everyday creativity reported benefits of mindfulness, resilience, collaboration with others, and self-awareness.

Updating the Discussion on Creativity and Well-being

Over the past few decades, a new field has emerged within psychology: positive psychology. Positive psychology re-examines universal truths (money doesn't buy happiness, life without love is empty, etc.) using scientific research methods, and, in a somewhat radical way, has shifted psychology's focus from mental illness to mental flourishing. The movement stresses applied research, extending its findings outside of academia to create practical, impactful change. The positive psychology movement, founded by Martin Seligman and Mihalyi Csikszentmihalyi (2000), has made its way globally into education, organizations, and governments.

Positive psychology updated the science of well-being for the 21st century, and with this new understanding comes a need to re-examine the place of creativity within this discussion. Recent advances in the research on well-being include a threshold of positive emotions that lead to flourishing or languishing, and new models of the "good life." Seligman (2012), the aforementioned positive psychology co-founder, proposed five elements of well-being: *positive emotion, engagement, positive relationships, meaning,* and *accomplishment or achievement* (PERMA). These five elements, vital to flourishing, also have strong ties to creativity. Positive relationships and creative collaboration, for example, can be seen as related concepts. This model is perhaps the most respected within the field of positive psychology, therefore this paper will use PERMA as a framework to update the discussion of creativity and well-being, taking into account the latest positive psychology research.

Positive Emotion

Fleeting or otherwise, emotions have profound, long-lasting effects on well-being, as evidenced in Fredrickson and Losada's (2005) research on the "positivity ratio" (ratio of positive to negative emotions). In their studies, Fredrickson and Losada found a tipping point of 3:1—flourishing individuals had a positivity ratio above 3:1 (on average 3.2:1 and 3.4:1 in the two samples), while languishing individuals had a positivity ratio below 3:1 (an average of 2.3:1 and 2.1:1; p. 685).

But where does positive emotion feature in creativity? May (1975) wrote, "There is a curiously sharp sense of joy—or perhaps better expressed, a sense of mild ecstasy—that comes when you find the particular form required by your creation" (pp. 122-123). Csikszentmihalyi (1996) speculated that the positive emotions related to creativity stem from evolution:

> No earthly builder could anticipate the kind of new situations the species might encounter tomorrow, the next year, or in the next decade, so the best program would be one that makes the species feel good whenever something new is discovered, regardless of its present usefulness. Evolution may have given humans such a program. (p. 108)

Fredrickson's (2004, 2013) "broaden and build theory" argued that positive emotions actually enlarge awareness: "Your awareness narrows with negative emotions and broadens with positive ones. It's when feeling good, then, that you're best equipped to see holistically and come up with creative and practical solutions to the problems you and others are facing" (Fredrickson, 2013, p. 82). Fredrickson's (2004, 2013) research found that positive emotions both "broaden" one's awareness and "build" one's resources—two essentials for creativity (in addition to well-being).

Engagement

The concept of *flow,* conceived by Csikszentmihalyi (1991), a psychologist and co-founder of positive psychology, referred to a state in which a person becomes totally absorbed in an activity, experiencing a loss of the sense of self, as well as a sense of timelessness. The level of challenge and skill are a match, bringing about a heightened focus that is highly enjoyable. To give a real-life example, Zen Buddhist priest and photographer Loori (2004) recounted,

> I was looking at the ground, navigating over big roots with the heavy camera on my shoulder. I looked up and saw a tree standing a few feet away and off to my right which riveted my attention.... Something about the way the light spilled over it drew me nearer. I approached it, bowed, set up my camera, and sat down on the ground next to the tripod.... I sat still and quietly as I could, with my hand on the shutter release. Briefly, I wondered how I was supposed to know when to make the exposure. That's the last thing I remember. Hours later, I realized I was shivering. The sun had set behind the mountains and the afternoon had turned cold. Somehow, time had vanished for me. I slowly rose, aware that something deep inside me had shifted.... I felt buoyant and joyful. (p. 20)

Loori achieved (1) a loss of sense of self, and (2) timelessness, the same results reported by those in flow. Consistent with Loori's joyfulness, those who regularly achieve flow report greater well-being (Csikszentmihalyi, 1991).

The flow state is more likely to occur when the activity is one the individual enjoys for its own sake, rather than for some extrinsic purpose (Csikszentmihalyi, 1991). This finds a direct connection in research about the motivation to be creative. Amabile's (1989) "creativity intersection" (p. 63) finds creative behavior occurring where creativity skills, task skills, and intrinsic motivation meet. According to Amabile (1983) and others (e.g., Deci, Koestner, & Ryan, 2001; Hennessey & Amabile, 1988), intrinsic motivation generally inspires creativity whereas extrinsic motivation inhibits creativity.

Positive Relationships

Emotional resources—love and meaningful relationships—expand and grow with positive emotions. As Fredrickson (2013) explained, when we experience positive emotions, we are more easily able to seek out and nourish these relationships that are so vital to well-being. Ultimately, an upward cycle of well-being results: positive emotions lead to more positive interactions, leading to more positive emotions, and so on.

When we look at positive relationships and their role in creativity, we begin with the recognition that much creativity is accomplished in groups. Johnson (2010) stated,

> The trick to creativity is not to sit around in glorious isolation and think big thoughts. The trick is to get more parts on the table.... A key way to get more parts on the table is to put yourself in networks of other creatives striving for the same thing...because they expose a wide and diverse sample of spare parts—mechanical or conceptual—and they encourage novel ways of recombining those parts. (p. 94)

Does working in a group with the mission of producing creative outcomes require positive relationships? Ekvall's (1996) dimensions of a creative climate include factors such as trust and openness, playfulness and humor, and debates. Among Ekvall's ten dimensions, the only one that is negatively correlated is conflict. In a similar vein, research shows that the highest-performing teams are those that—in addition to having certain expected traits such as sharing a meaningful purpose and having an agreed-upon working approach—also are deeply committed to one another's personal growth and success (Katzenbach & Smith, 1994).

Close collaboration is making its way into the workplace with innovative companies such as the design firm IDEO, companies that recognize the importance—even the necessity—of social cohesion in collaboration. They advise, "Leaving your personal life out of your professional life takes a toll on creative thought.... Each person on your team brings unique life experiences to the table.... Make it a priority to hang out and get to know each other. Having fun together will improve your collaboration" (Kelley & Kelley, 2013, p. 191).

Encouraged by companies such as IDEO, collaborative networks can function as professional and personal support networks simultaneously. As Almond (2012) playfully remarked,

> A generation ago, when *Annie Hall* won the Oscar for Best Picture, talk therapy occupied a prominent place in our collective imagination, whether or not you partook. If you wanted to spend several hours a week baring your soul to a stranger who was professionally obligated to listen and react, you went to therapy. Today you join a writing workshop. (para. 7)

Robinson (2009) calls this unique creative support network a "tribe." As Robinson pointed out, "What connects a tribe is a common commitment to the thing they feel born to do. This can be extremely liberating, especially if you've been pursuing your passion alone" (p. 105).

Meaning

In his research on creative personality, Csikszentmihalyi (1996) found that:

> creative individuals don't have to be dragged out of bed; they are eager
> to start the day. This is not because they are cheerful, enthusiastic types.
> Nor do they necessarily have something exciting to do. But they believe
> that there is something meaningful to accomplish each day, and they
> can't wait to get started on it. (p. 349)

The earlier discussion of intrinsic motivation barely scratched the surface of
what is known about intrinsic motivation as a driver of creative behavior. Pink
(2011) broke down the sources of intrinsic motivation into three, one of which is
purpose. (The other two are autonomy and mastery.) If one subscribes to Pink's
theory of motivation, a sense of purpose (or meaning) leads to greater creativity
and productivity in our current era: "It's in our nature to seek purpose. But that
nature is now being revealed and expressed on a scale that is demographically
unprecedented and, until recently, scarcely imaginable. The consequences could
rejuvenate our business and remake our world" (p. xi).

Accomplishment/Achievement

Positive psychology takes a strengths-based approach to human flourishing, rather
than considering achievement merely to be the reaching of specific outcomes.
In areas such as education and psychotherapy, positive psychology encourages
individuals to identify and find ways to use their signature strengths. Seligman
(2012) characterizes a signature strength as providing:

> a sense of ownership and authenticity...a feeling of excitement while
> displaying it...a rapid learning curve as the strength is practiced, a
> sense of yearning to find new ways to use it, a feeling of inevitability
> in using the strength...invigoration rather than exhaustion while using
> the strength, the creation and pursuit of personal projects that revolve
> around it, joy, zest, enthusiasm, even ecstasy while using it. (pp. 38-39)

While creative people are often focused on an end product (product being one
of the well-known 4 Ps of creativity, along with person, process, and press;
Rhodes, 1961), living creatively is often seen as a worthy goal of its own, separate from any specific achievement (e.g., Maslow, 1971; May, 1975). Maslow
(1962/1998) said, "Every human being has the instinctive need for the highest
values of beauty, truth, and justice, and so on. If we can accept this notion, then
the key question isn't 'what fosters creativity?' But it is why in God's name isn't
everyone creative?" (p. 11).

The PERMA Model (Expanded)

Huppert and So of the University of Cambridge employed a similar but broader model as compared to Seligman's in their work measuring the well-being of countries (as cited in Seligman, 2012). Digging more deeply, they include three additional characteristics of well-being: *resilience, vitality,* and *self-determination.*

Resilience

Creativity demands resilience and vice versa. In terms of daily life, creativity "helps each person to cope with hassles, express him- or herself, and adjust to changes. Not a day goes by, and perhaps not an hour, without the need for adjustment" (Runco, 1997, p. 93). When engaging in the creative process, one rarely emerges unscathed, particularly during the prototyping stages when failure is virtually guaranteed.

The cycle of prototyping (creating a prototype, soliciting feedback, improving the prototype, soliciting feedback, etc.) brings about resilience and—perhaps unexpectedly—optimism. Experiencing this process of small failures, which lead to small successes, which lead to big successes, bolsters optimism. As argued by Kelley and Kelley (2013) in *Creative Confidence:*

> Once you have gone through enough rapid innovation cycles, you will gain familiarity with process and confidence in your ability to assess new ideas. And that confidence results in reduced anxiety in the face of ambiguity when you are bringing new ideas into the world. (p. 49)

Positive emotion can help in embracing failure and coping with mistakes. Fredrickson's (2004) aforementioned "broaden and build theory" asserts that positive emotions build resiliency and lessen any "lingering negative emotion" (p. 1371) toward past failure or trauma. Naturally, positive affect builds one's ability to persist through setbacks and failures in the creative process.

Essentially, creativity provides a valuable emotional skill that helps with difficult situations through optimism and perseverance. Likewise, those who show resiliency in other areas of their lives are more apt to integrate these skills into their creative process.

Vitality

High energy, spontaneity, and enthusiasm are common traits among creative individuals (Davis, 2004). They become intensely focused on the problems or projects they are working on, compelled to see them through to the end. They also tend to seek out novel and stimulating experiences, despite the potential risks.

Furthermore, to quote Csikszentmihalyi (1996), "The...reason creativity is so fascinating is that when we are involved in it, we feel that we are living more fully than during the rest of life" (p. 2). Creative vitality might be seen as a cycle: creative people possess vitality, inspiring them to create. In turn, creativity can be a deeply joyful experience, inspiring a sense of vitality.

Self-determination

To accomplish their work, creative individuals often follow strict, almost religious, rituals. The book *Daily Rituals* (Currey, 2013) chronicles hundreds of prolific creators and the rituals that helped to make them so. Applying structure and habit to creative work takes a great deal of self-determination, especially in solo creative work.

Ultimately, the most creative individuals are often also the most prolific in their work. "Pablo Picasso produced about twenty thousand pieces of art. Albert Einstein wrote more than 240 scientific papers.... Richard Branson started 250 companies" (Sawyer, 2013, p. 129). Not every painting, paper, or company was a success. Rather, through trial and error, and producing a large body of work from which to draw, a small margin of their work succeeded and ultimately determined their fame.

Limits

In *The Paradox of Choice,* Schwartz (2004) described how, contrary to assumptions, increased choice does not necessarily lead to increased happiness. Increased choice causes dissatisfaction for a number of reasons such as regret, greater awareness of opportunity costs, and heightened expectations. In a simple study of jam, Schwartz demonstrated how people react to choice in counterintuitive ways. In one scenario, six jams were offered for sampling, while in another scenario twenty-four were offered. In both cases, all twenty-four varieties were available for purchase. In the condition with six available varieties to sample, thirty percent of shoppers purchased jam, while in the condition with twenty-four available varieties to sample, a minuscule three percent made a purchase. The lesson from this study is that in terms of satisfaction, less can be more. And the same is true for life satisfaction: in many cases, the fewer choices over which to anguish, the greater the contentment with the one chosen.

Creativity, which as a discipline favors abundance over scarcity, paradoxically thrives upon limits. In a sense, limits allow creativity to happen; they define creativity in that creativity often means manipulating limits in a previously unforeseen way. Famous choreographer Twyla Tharp (2003) found that having too many resources—an unlimited budget, rehearsal time, etc.—actually hinders her creativity. In her book *The Creative Habit,* Tharp wrote, "Whom the gods wish to destroy, they give unlimited resources" (p. 129). Johnson (2010) wrote about "the adjacent possible," showing how innovation happens when the accepted boundaries are expanded into what's currently possible, a space that is not unlimited.

Putting It into Practice: Methods to Increase Your Creativity and Well-being

Research has proven that both creativity and positive emotion can be enhanced through deliberate practice (e.g., Scott, Leritz, & Mumford, 2004; Seligman, 2006). In his book, *Learned Optimism,* Seligman (2006) determined, true to the title, that optimism can be learned (as can helplessness): "Pessimists can learn the skills of optimism and permanently improve the quality of their lives.... Becoming an optimist consists...simply of learning a set of skills about how to talk to *yourself* when you suffer a personal defeat" (p. 208).

If optimism is a skill, it requires practice—and creativity is in many ways the ideal training. During the early ideation phase, expressing negative judgments towards ideas cuts off the flow, potentially discouraging individuals from offering ideas that might be rejected. When assessing ideas, too, it is important to point out both positive and negative aspects, to be constructive while being realistic. One way to critique an idea without crushing it is to first point out the positives and then make suggestions. The creativity tool POINt—Pluses, Opportunities, Issues, and New thinking (ways to overcome the issues)—helps groups converge in a positive way (Miller, Vehar, Firestien, Thurber, & Nielsen, 2011).

As mentioned earlier, the planning and prototyping phases force one to learn lessons in resilience. Developing a novel idea will involve risk and thus potential failure, which necessitates continuous optimism and resilience as setbacks occur. Kelley and Kelley (2013) argued that through experiencing these failures, coping with them, and emerging with a creation (whether or not it resembles the initial vision), creative confidence is the outcome. The resilience developed in the creative process translates, then, to resilience in difficult life events.

Finally, Fredrickson (2013) showed that people can experience more love, which she defines as a shared positive emotion, through practices such as *loving kindness meditation*. Experiencing more of these moments has far-reaching effects, as she explained:

> When people, completely new to meditation, learned to quiet their minds and expand their capacity for love and kindness, they transformed themselves from the inside out. They experienced more love, more engagement, more serenity, more joy, more amusement—more of every positive emotion we measured.... Their lives spiraled upward. The kindheartedness they learned to stoke during their meditation practices warmed their connection with others. (Fredrickson, 2013, p. 12)

This research is based in biology, showing that loving kindness meditation can actually change people's physical makeup, such as increasing vagal tone (the vagus nerve connects the brain to the heart).

Conclusion

Through rigorous research and concrete tools, positive psychology expands the discussion of well-being and creativity beyond self-actualization, the creative person, and everyday creativity. With the work of positive psychologists, there is a new language to discuss creativity and well-being, such as the broaden and build theory (Fredrickson, 2004, 2013), flow (Csikszentmihalyi, 1991), and the positivity ratio (Fredrickson & Losada, 2005). Furthermore, as evidenced through the framework of PERMA (Seligman, 2012), creativity offers a path to fulfilling the elements determined by positive psychologists as leading the "good life": positive emotion, engagement, positive relationships, meaning, and accomplishment or achievement.

Creativity, under the umbrella of positive psychology, offers sound wisdom and concrete tools for living a healthier, fuller life. So, when the need for a creativity book arises, there is an obvious place to look.

References

Almond, S. (2012, March 23). *Why talk therapy is on the wane and writing workshops are on the rise.* Retrieved from http://www.nytimes.com/2012/03/25/magazine/why-talk-therapy-is-on-the-wane-and-writing-workshops-are-on-the-rise.html?_r=0

Amabile, T. M. (1983). *The social psychology of creativity.* New York, NY: Springer-Verlag.

Amabile, T. M. (1989). *Growing up creative.* New York, NY: Crown.

Csikszentmihalyi, M. (1991). *Flow: The psychology of optimal experience.* New York, NY: HarperPerennial.

Csikszentmihalyi, M. (1996). *Creativity: Flow and the psychology of discovery and invention.* New York, NY: Harper Collins Publishers.

Currey, M. (2013) *Daily rituals: How artists work.* New York, NY: Alfred A. Knopf.

Davis, G. A. (2004). *Creativity is forever* (5th ed.). Dubuque, IA: Kendall/Hunt Publishing Company.

Deci, E. L., Koestner, R., & Ryan, R. M. (2001). Extrinsic rewards and intrinsic motivation in education: Reconsidered once again. *Review of Educational Research, 71,* 1-27.

Ekvall, G. (1996). Organizational climate for creativity and innovation. *European Journal of Work and Organizational Psychology, 5*(1), 105-123.

Fredrickson, B. L. (2004). The broaden-and-build theory of positive emotions. *Philosophical Transactions of the Royal Society B: Biological Sciences, 359*(1449), 1367-1378.

Fredrickson, B. L. (2013). *Love 2.0.* New York, NY: Penguin Group.

Fredrickson, B. L., & Losada, M. F. (2005). Positive affect and the complex dynamics of human flourishing. *American Psychologist, 60*(7), 678-686.

Hennessey, B. A., & Amabile, T. M. (1998). Reward, intrinsic motivation, and creativity. *American Psychologist, 53,* 674-675.

Johnson, S. (2010). *Where good ideas come from: The natural history of innovation.* New York, NY: Penguin Group.

Katzenbach, J. R., & Smith, D. K. (1994). *The wisdom of teams: Creating a high-performance organization.* New York, NY: HarperCollins.

Kelley, D., & Kelley, T. (2013). *Creative confidence: Unleashing the creative potential within us all*. New York, NY: Random House.

Loori, J. D. (2004). *The Zen of creativity*. New York, NY: Random House.

Maslow, A. H. (1998). *Maslow on management*. New York, NY: Wiley. (Original work published 1962)

Maslow, A. H. (1971). *The farther reaches of human nature*. New York, NY: Viking Press.

May, R. (1975). *The courage to create*. New York, NY: W.W. Norton & Company.

Miller, B., Vehar, J. R., Firestien, R. L., Thurber, S., & Nielsen, D. (2011). *Creativity unbound: An introduction to creative process* (5th ed.). Evanston, IL: FourSight, LLC.

Osteen, J. (2008). *Your best life begins each morning: Devotions to start every day of the year*. New York, NY: FaithWords.

Pink, D. (2011). *Drive: The surprising truth about what motivates us*. New York, NY: Riverhead Books.

Rhodes, M. (1961). An analysis of creativity. *Phi Delta Kappan, 42*(7), 305-310.

Robinson, K. (2009). *The element: How finding your passion changes everything*. New York, NY: Penguin Group.

Runco, M. A. (1997). To understand is to create: An epistemological perspective on human nature and personal creativity. In M. A. Runco & R. Richards (Eds.), *Eminent creativity, everyday creativity, and health* (pp. 91-108). Washington, DC: American Psychological Association.

Sawyer, K. (2013). *Zig zag: The surprising path to greater creativity*. San Francisco, CA: Jossey-Bass.

Schwartz, B. (2004). *The paradox of choice: Why more is less*. New York, NY: HarperCollins.

Scott, G., Leritz, L. E., & Mumford, M. D. (2004). The effectiveness of creativity training: A quantitative review. *Creativity Research Journal, 16*(4), 361-388.

Seligman, M. E. (2006). *Learned optimism: How to change your mind and your life*. New York, NY: Vintage Books.

Seligman, M. E. (2012). *Flourish: A visionary new understanding of happiness and well-being*. New York, NY: Simon and Schuster.

Seligman, M. E., & Csikszentmihalyi, M. (2000). Positive psychology: An introduction. *American Psychologist, 55*(1), 6-14.

Tharp, T. (2003). *The creative habit: Learn it and use it for life.* New York, NY: Simon & Schuster.

Tolle, E. (1999). *The power of now: A guide to spiritual enlightenment.* Novato, CA: New World Library.

About the Author

Molly Holinger holds a Master of Science in Creativity from the International Center for Studies in Creativity at SUNY Buffalo State. She is a former ICSC graduate assistant and a former creativity teaching assistant and research assistant at the University of Illinois Urbana-Champaign. She is currently pursuing a Ph.D. in Educational Psychology at the University of Connecticut. Her publications include "The Creative Religion" in *Stone Voices Magazine,* and the textbook *Building Your Creativity.*

LinkedIn: https://www.linkedin.com/in/molly-holinger-a3a57175

How Can Spiritual Intelligence Help Us Cultivate Creative Potential?

Rebecca DiLiberto
International Center for Studies in Creativity
SUNY Buffalo State

Abstract

The nature and nurture of human potential, intellectual abilities, and creative achievements have long been topics of interest in the science of human behavior. In particular, there is an emerging effort to understand the relationship between spiritual intelligence and creativity. Research suggests that developing our spiritual intelligence is quite relevant to the cultivation of our creative potentials. There appears to be a current desire by many people for a higher intellectual level of spirituality, and an eagerness to learn how to develop creative potentials, enhance one's senses of purpose, and deepen one's connections to the world. The purpose of this paper is to provide a comprehensive and contemporary overview of spiritual intelligence, and the relationship of spiritual intelligence to creativity and one's sense of purpose and meaning.

How Can Spiritual Intelligence Help Us Cultivate Creative Potential?

T here is an imbalance in the forms of intelligences recognized by our culture. General intelligence (often measured as an intelligence quotient, or IQ) is perceived as the predominant form of intelligence, outweighing less tangible abilities and intelligences such as visual-spatial intelligence (Gardner, 1983), emotional intelligence (EQ; Goleman, 1995), spiritual intelligence (SQ; Zohar, 2000), creative thinking ability, and others. This imbalance is compounded with Western cultural values such as immediate gratification and the "quest to be the best." The result is a narrowed perspective on the importance of these other intelligences and abilities—and, in the case of SQ, a discounting of its value. Meanwhile, there is a culturally-driven yearning to find a purposeful life. People in all walks of life appear not only to desire and appreciate a higher intellectual level of spirituality, but are eager to learn how to cultivate their creative potentials, enhance their senses of purpose, and deepen their connections to the world.

Contemporary literature and scholarly opinion suggest that SQ is a vital and valid form of intelligence, which can influence creative achievement and enhance a sense of life purpose. But have we fallen for the misconception of defining creativity, spirituality, and intelligence as mutually exclusive? How might SQ influence creativity? With these questions in mind, the primary overarching question to address is: Are we developing our SQ to cultivate our creative potentials and senses of life's meaning? The intent of this paper is to explore the concept of SQ and discuss how it is related to creativity and enhancing one's sense of purpose and meaning in the world.

Spiritual Intelligence

The concept of SQ is rooted in the idea of spirituality. Spirituality is distinct from religion in that it encompasses universal domains of humanity and is not confined to religious practices or beliefs (Elkins, Hedstrom, Hughes, Leaf, & Saunders, 1988; Wigglesworth, 2012). The wide range of understanding surrounding spirituality has influenced its definition. Spirituality has been associated with terms ranging from *supernatural* to *the essence of being* (King, 2005; Sriraman, 2009). In line with the humanistic understanding of spirituality, and most congruent with the concept of SQ, Wigglesworth (2012) defined spirituality as "the innate human need to be connected to something larger than ourselves, something we consider to be divine or of exceptional nobility" (p. 8).

Contemporary SQ Ideologies

The various views and interpretations of spirituality contribute to the diversity of SQ ideologies. Many studies, theories, and definitions of SQ have been developed and applied to the fields of academics, business, and leadership. However, primary characteristics of SQ have emerged from the literature to form the contemporary ideology (Table 1).

Perhaps due to the many primary characteristics of SQ, it remains controversial if SQ is truly an independent and measurable intelligence. It is nevertheless instructive to consider what some scholars have said about SQ: it is intimately related with creativity; creativity is an important and fundamental aspect in the nurturing of SQ; and the components of SQ strongly complement our quests for deep self-awareness, appreciation for inner knowing, higher states of consciousness, universal interconnectedness, and insight into existential questions for attaining meaningful goals and a sense of purpose (Emmons, 2000a, 2000b; Green & Noble, 2010; Noble, 2009; Sinetar, 1992, 2000; Vaughan, 2002; Wigglesworth, 2012; Zohar & Marshall, 2000, 2004). The contemporary ideology of SQ is primarily influenced by humanistic and transpersonal psychology, paying strong tribute to the spiritual natures of transcendent experience and "plateau experience" (Maslow, 1971, p. 281). Such experiences are thought to be of great importance in encouraging greater well-being, self-actualization, and creative and spiritual growth. Accordingly, engaging in problem solving, observing continuous spiritual and creative thinking practices, and practicing leadership should simultaneously nurture both SQ and creativity. Therefore, it is reasonable to think that developing SQ is highly relevant to developing one's creative potential.

Sisk and Torrance (2001) developed a comprehensive and holistic understanding of SQ that is representative of contemporary ideology and of the relationship between SQ and creativity. They associated the essence of SQ to a deep self-awareness and an inner experience of the continuously-evolving self. They explained, "A person leading a spiritual life wants to feel connected, to feel a sense of community, to be free of restrictions, to experience inner freedom and a life of meaning" (p. 8). Through the expression of SQ, they continued, one becomes more aware of the inner processes of the self to develop and nurture higher values, motivations, intentions, and aspirations. More conclusively, Sisk and Torrance highlighted four areas that resonate with the authentic meaning and concept of SQ: *inner knowing, deep intuition, oneness with nature and the universe,* and *problem solving*. The following sections will explore how these focal areas are related and can influence one's creativity.

Inner Knowing

"Inner knowing is to know the essence of consciousness and to realize that this inner essence is the essence of all creation" (Sisk & Torrance, 2001, p. 11).

Without our conscious awareness, our imaginations, creativity, intelligences, and senses of self are void. Our abilities to reflect on the past, to be mindful of the present, and to imagine the future are dependent on our different levels of consciousness. "To achieve a life filled with meaning, you must figure out how to be more conscious; only then do you become the author of your own destiny" (Chopra & Tanzi, 2012, p. 57). Inner knowing can strengthen our ability to unlock different levels of consciousness, to listen to our intuition, to problem-solve life's big questions, and to direct our creative potentials toward a meaningful life.

Inner knowing is often associated with intuition, gut feeling, inner voice, or sense of self (Burnett, 2010), but it is not to be confused with deep intuition. Vaughan (1979) explained how intuitive experiences could funnel into physical, emotional, mental, and spiritual levels of awareness. *Physical intuition* refers to body responses, sensations, and conscious awareness of one's physical being and surrounding environment. *Emotional intuition* is concerned with empathy, feelings, and a heightened ability to recognize synchronicity experiences. *Mental intuition* is associated with creativity, problem solving, imagery, and the process where unconscious patterns become conscious. Each of these are associated with inner knowing. However, the fourth form of awareness—*spiritual intuition*—is more closely associated with deep intuition. Vaughan wrote, "Pure, spiritual intuition is distinguished from other forms by its independence from sensations, feelings, and thoughts" (p. 77).

Having faith in one's intuitions is an important quality of SQ, creative thinking, and problem solving. Interestingly, Kaufman (2013) found that faith in intuition, superstitious thinking, and impractical expectations "are not always irrational.... They are often conducive to reaching one's goals.... Faith in intuition is associated with a reduced latent inhibition, which in turn, is associated with higher levels of creative achievement" (p. 304). Burnett (2010, 2014) advocated intuition and mindfulness as being prevalent throughout the Creative Problem Solving (CPS) process, with particular attention drawn to the affective skills. Mindfulness in CPS allows for a greater awareness of intuition, and helps to balance the ebb and flow of the affective and cognitive skills. Hence, the intuition in inner knowing, embedded in SQ, does not replace one's creative thinking skills, but works as an internal resource influencing change along one's spiritual creative journey.

Table 1. *SQ Ideologies Primary Characteristics*

SQ Primary Characteristics	Emmons, 2000a, 2000b	Green & Noble, 2010; Noble, 2009	Sinetar, 1992, 2000	Vaughan, 2002	Wigglesworth, 2012	Zohar & Marshall, 2000, 2004
Abilities to Nurture & Develop	X	X	X	X	X	X
Creativity is Fundamental			X	X		X
Creativity Relevance/Associations	X	X	X	X	X	X
Existential Questions/Thinking	X	X	X	X	X	X
Higher Conscious Expansion	X	X	X	X	X	X
Humanistic/Transpersonal Psychology Influence	X	X	X	X	X	X
Codependent Intelligence					X	
Measurable					X	X

SQ Ideologies

Primary Characteristic						
Personal Meaning/Purpose	X	X	X	X	X	X
Problem Solving	X	X	X	X	X	X
Psychological Health Well-being	X	X	X	X	X	
Self-Awareness/Inner Knowing	X	X	X	X	X	X
Spiritual Change Agent/Leadership		X	X		X	X
Spiritual Practitioner	X	X	X	X	X	X
Spiritual/Transcendent/Plateau Experiences	X	X	X	X	X	X
Transcendental Awareness/Capacity	X	X	X	X	X	X
Universal Awareness/Interconnectedness	X	X	X	X	X	X

Note: Cells with an X denote when authors included the corresponding primary characteristic in their SQ ideology.

Deep Intuition

SQ assists in overlooking the egotistical self to employ deep intuition in developing solutions for the greater good (Sisk & Torrance, 2001).

Deep intuition in many aspects fits Vaughan's (1979) definition of spiritual intuition, Harman's (1988) M-3 Transcendental Monism (from his three metaphysical perspectives), and Jung's (1959/1980) concept of the collective unconscious. Each author discussed how our rational minds could hinder our ability to access higher states of consciousness that transcend true awakening. It is at this level that consciousness transcends the sense of self, ego, or the concept of "I."

Deep intuition strongly contributes to self-actualization. To foster deep intuition, one must seek experiences of spiritual growth to remove the clutter and suppressed creative energy from all levels of consciousness. Csikszentmihalyi (1990) included forms of this throughout his lists of attributes prevalent during optimal or flow experiences; for instance, concentration on the task at hand; the removal of anxiety from the mind, and the loss of self-consciousness; and the loss of inhibitions and consciousness of the self. Flow or peak experiences can result in rewarding and lasting impressions, due to their spiritual natures (Csikszentmihalyi & Rathunde, 1990). Noble (2000) has even argued that spiritual experiences not only facilitate self-actualizations but are precursors to spiritual intelligence. Deep intuition assists in the process of self-actualization through the production of spiritual and transcendent experiences, and integrates one's unrestricted creativity with the collective being.

Through deep intuition, one has the capability to reach beyond self-actualization and strengthen one's potential for self-transcendence. Rogers (1979) believed that every individual has actualizing tendencies, and that the knowledge and experiences of our authentic consciences impact our personas. He stated, "we are tuning in to a potent creative tendency which has formed our universe.... And perhaps we are touching the cutting edge of our ability to transcend ourselves, to create new and more spiritual directions in human evolution" (p. 8).

Maslow's efforts to promote creativity are evident in his concept of self-actualization. His insights into spirituality are further heightened in his Theory Z, with the spiritual nature of the "plateau experience" and transcending self-actualizers (Maslow, 1971, p. 281). Maslow further proposed that self-actualized transcenders exceed the expectation of self-actualized non-transcenders. Feuerstein (1997) wrote that self-actualized transcenders "are motivated by the desire to realize their true identity, which is the identity of all beings and things—the transcendental Self" (p. 139).

With the support of deep intuition in SQ, one can transcend the ego, past unconscious notions and the illusion of reality, to direct his or her potential and cultivate solutions in benefit of the greater good.

Oneness with Nature and the Universe

SQ harmonizes with nature and the world around us to find a purpose in life that is intrinsically motivating (Sisk & Torrance, 2001).

Everything is a process, from nature and the universe to spirituality and creativity. The quest for spiritual and creative growth becomes vital when life's processes and motivations start to become unbalanced. Oneness with nature and the universe "urges us to search for wholeness, a sense of community and relationship, to create an identity, and to search for meaning; and out of this search for meaning will come a sense of empowerment" (Sisk & Torrance, 2001, p. 12).

To live a creative life of meaning, an individual must venture into the realms of his inner world in conjunction with the outer world (Robinson & Aronica, 2013). According to Amabile (1997), "maintaining your own creativity in your work depends on maintaining your intrinsic motivation" (p. 55). In many creative endeavors, inspiration is a key component in maintaining intrinsic motivation (Kaufman, 2013) and orchestrating SQ (Sinetar, 2000; Vaughan, 2002). Creative inspiration transpires in the outer world of the self and often provokes an intuitive sense of opening, an awakening of new perceptions, and a connection to one's inner world (Kaufman, 2013; Rogers, 1961). Vaughan (2002) explained that SQ "facilitates the integration of subjective insights and illuminations with ways of being and acting in the world" (p. 7). In the end, our individual pursuits of meaning and purpose are lost without the connection to each other and the world. Csikszentmihalyi (1990) explained:

> Just as we have learned to separate ourselves from each other and from the environment, we now need to learn how to reunite ourselves with the other entities around us without losing our hard-won individuality. The most promising faith for the future might be based on the realization that the entire universe is a system related by common laws and that it makes no sense to impose our dreams and desires on nature without taking them into account. Recognizing the limitations of human will, accepting a cooperative rather than a ruling role in the universe, we should feel the relief of the exile who is finally returning home. The problem of meaning will then be resolved as the individual's purpose merges with the universal flow. (p. 240)

We are a trivial part of an infinite world and universal process that is far greater than ourselves. Looking at our place in the universe guides the attitudes of openness to novelty and tolerance for ambiguity and complexity, to put our problems into perspective. In turn, this generates novel ideas and cultivates meaningful solutions for the purpose of a collective ambition (Quarrie, 2015). The oneness with nature and the universe component of SQ complements and guides our internal creative processes and our senses of purpose and meaning to the external world.

Problem Solving

SQ guides one's life's purpose and meaning throughout the entire problem solving process (Sisk & Torrance, 2001).

Problem solving and change is an inevitable occurrence in human life, and could even be thought of as the entire process of being alive, with our selves as the evolving innovative solutions. SQ "is not amoral, it engages us in questions of good and evil and affords us opportunities to dream, to reconfigure, to look beyond the boundaries of a situation to what it could be" (Sisk & Torrance, 2001, p. 12). Not only do we ask questions of meaning and purpose in hopes to put our lives in perspective, but these perceptions, behaviors, and motivations have powerful influences in the world around us. SQ provides insight into harmonizing one's sense of purpose and peace across multiple life contexts in the pursuit of generating creative change for the world.

Creativity is change, thus it can easily be argued that the great spiritual warriors were not just change agents but *creative* change agents. Mahatma Gandhi, Nelson Mandela, Martin Luther King Jr., and Mother Teresa were solving problems with meaning and value to the world, not just to themselves. They embodied the spirit of creativity within their own SQ. As Sisk and Torrance (2001) wrote, SQ "has the capacity to integrate these intelligences and enable them to achieve the highest realization of human nature" (p. 7). At this point creativity becomes a way of living and being, "the force that drives all life" (Chopra & Chopra, 2011, p. 119). SQ arguably is the necessary and overarching intelligence of CPS.

In addition to creative spiritual warriors internalizing the principles of creativity, three qualities remain primary: love, wisdom, and compassion. According to Wigglesworth's (2012) research on SQ, love is comprised of wisdom and compassion. Love nurtures creativity within ourselves and others. Wisdom and compassion allow love and creativity to flourish and extend human meaning and purpose towards a greater good. In relation to creativity, love is commonly associated with the internal desire or passion that propels an individual's creative ability (Amabile, 1997; Sternberg, 1988; Torrance, 1995). And wisdom in creativity can be linked with the importance of a positive attitude, knowledge, and evaluation supported by a vision and deliberate practice (Parnes, Noller, & Biondi, 1977; Puccio, Mance, Barbero Switalski, & Reali, 2012). On the other hand, there seems to be little emphasis on the direct connection between creativity and compassion. To be compassionate is "to suffer with another; sympathy for the suffering of others, often including a desire to help" (Dossey, 2007, p. 1). The strongest component of compassion is the desire to help; this motivation alone proactively promotes imagination, creative thinking, problem solving, and leadership. Correspondingly, Kaufman (2013) researched creative achievement and openness to experience, finding correlations with compassion. With these ideas in mind, compassion—and even the combination of love, wisdom, and compassion—may warrant further research to heighten the instrumental correlation between SQ, creativity, CPS, and creative leadership.

Nurturing the Creative, Spiritual Life

All humans are innately spiritual and creative, and have the ability to deliberately strengthen those natural tendencies or let them weaken. As one focuses on nurturing one's own creative potential, it is important to remember that accessing one's inner awareness, personal obstacles, and individual processes are driving forces in the progression and direction of growth. Taking the time to practice inner knowing, deep intuition, oneness with nature and the universe, and problem solving to harmonize the creative being is a spiritual journey of continuous transformation. In an effort to guide one's spiritual, creative journey, Sisk and Torrance's (2001) suggest seven ways to nurture and develop SQ:

1. Think about your goals, desires and wants, to bring your life into perspective and balance, and identify your values.

2. Access your inner processes and use visualization to see your goals, desires and wants fulfilled, and experience the emotion connected with this fulfillment.

3. Integrate your personal and universal vision and recognize your connectedness to others, to nature, to the world, and to the universe.

4. Take responsibility for your goals, desires, and wants.

5. Develop a sense of community by letting more people into your life.

6. Focus on love and compassion.

7. When chance knocks at your door, let it in and take advantage of coincidences. (p. 180)

It is through the development and understanding of these SQ ambitions that we can reawaken our inner compasses to direct our creative potentials and guide our paths to self-actualization, self-transcendence, and the greater good. Ultimately, this will allow us to lead more creative and spiritual lives of meaning and purpose. As one's sense of purpose and life direction evolves, so will one's spiritual, creative journey.

Conclusion

The nature and nurture of human potential, intellectual abilities, and creative achievements has long been a topic of interest in the science of human behavior. Many human behaviors and motivations are spiritual in nature, such as love, wisdom, compassion, inspiration, openness to experiences, self-actualization, and the cultivation of one's creative potentials. SQ is an oft-neglected but important type of intelligence that is related to both creativity and one's sense of purpose in life. Considerable scholarly works have helped shape and develop contemporary SQ ideology, as well as identify the components of SQ within all of us that are important in assisting self-actualization, creative potential, and the greater good. To nurture our SQ we must expose ourselves to experiences that best complement our unique creative natures. And to nurture our creative natures, we must expose ourselves to experiences that enhance our SQ.

References

Amabile, T. M. (1997). Motivating creativity in organizations: On doing what you love and loving what you do. *California Management Review, 40*(1), 39-58.

Burnett, C. (2010). *Holistic approaches to creative problem solving.* [Unpublished doctoral thesis.] Toronto, Canada: University of Toronto.

Burnett, C. (2014). The missing link: Teaching the creative problem solving process. In J. Piirto (Ed.), *Organic creativity in the classroom: Teaching to intuition in academics and the arts* (pp. 285-297). Waco, TX: Prufrock Press.

Chopra, D., & Chopra, G. (2011). *The seven spiritual laws of superheroes: Harnessing our power to change the world.* New York, NY: HarperCollins.

Chopra, D., & Tanzi, R. E. (2012). *Super brain: Unleashing the explosive power of your mind to maximize health, happiness, and spiritual well-being.* New York, NY: Crown Publishing Group.

Csikszentmihalyi, M. (1990). *Flow: The psychology of optimal experience.* New York, NY: HarperPerennial.

Csikszentmihalyi, M., & Rathunde, K. (1990). The psychology of wisdom: An evolutionary interpretation. In R. J. Sternberg (Ed.), *Wisdom: Its nature, origins, and development* (pp. 26-51). New York, NY: Cambridge University Press.

Dossey, D. (2007). Compassion. *EXPLORE: The Journal of Science and Healing, 3*(1), 1-5.

Elkins, D. N., Hedstrom, L. J., Hughes, L. L., Leaf, J. A., & Saunders, C. (1988). Toward a humanistic-phenomenological spirituality: Definition, description, and measurement. *Journal of Humanistic Psychology, 28*(4), 5-18.

Emmons, R. A. (2000a). Is spirituality an intelligence? Motivation, cognition, and the psychology of ultimate concern. *The International Journal for the Psychology of Religion, 10*(1), 3-26.

Emmons, R. A. (2000b). Spirituality and intelligence: Problems and prospects. *The International Journal for the Psychology of Religion, 10*(1), 57-64.

Feuerstein, G. (1997). *Lucid waking: Mindfulness and the spiritual potential of humanity.* Rochester, VT: Inner Traditions International.

Gardner, H. (1983). *Frames of mind: The theory of multiple intelligences.* New York, NY: Basic Books.

Goleman, D. (1995). Emotional intelligence: Why it can matter more than IQ. New York, NY: Bantam Books.

Green, W. N., & Noble, K. D. (2010). Fostering spiritual intelligence: Undergraduates' growth in a course about consciousness. *Advanced Development Journal, 12*(1), 26-49.

Harman, W. (1988). *Global mind change: The promise of the last years of the 20th century.* Indianapolis, IN: Knowledge Systems Inc.

Jung, C. G. (1980). *The archetypes and the collective unconscious* (2nd ed., R. F. C. Hull Trans.). Princeton, NJ: Princeton University Press. (Original work published 1959)

Kaufman, S. B. (2013). *Ungifted: Intelligence redefined.* Philadelphia, PA: Perseus Books Group.

King, P. (2005). Spirituality. In C. Fisher & R. Lerner (Eds.), *Encyclopedia of applied developmental science* (Vol. 2, pp. 1047-1047). Thousand Oaks, CA: Sage Publications.

Maslow, A. H. (1971). *The farther reaches of human nature.* New York, NY: Viking Press.

Noble, K. D. (2000). Spiritual intelligence: A new frame of mind. *Advanced Development, 9,* 1-29.

Noble, K. D. (2009). Spiritual intelligence. In B. Kerr (Ed.), *Encyclopedia of giftedness, creativity, and talent* (pp. 821-823). Thousand Oaks, CA: Sage Publications.

Parnes, S. J., Noller, R. B., & Biondi, A. M. (1977). *Guide to creative action.* New York, NY: Charles Scribner's Sons.

Puccio, G. J., Mance, M., Barbero Switalski, L., & Reali, P. D. (2012). *Creativity rising: Creative thinking and creative problem solving in the 21st century.* Buffalo, NY: ICSC Press.

Quarrie, J. A. (2015). How does nature nurture creativity? In M. K. Culpepper & C. Burnett (Eds.), *Big questions in creativity 2015* (pp. 93-112). Buffalo, NY: ICSC Press.

Robinson, K., & Aronica, L. (2013). *Finding your element: How to discover your talents and passions and transform your life.* New York, NY: Penguin.

Rogers, C. (1961). *On becoming a person: A therapist's view of psychotherapy.* Boston, MA: Houghton Mifflin.

Rogers, C. R. (1979). The foundations of the person-centered approach. *Education, 100*(2), 98-107.

Sinetar, M. (1992). *A way without words: A guide for spiritually emerging adults.* Mahwah, NJ: Paulist Press.

Sinetar, M. (2000). *Spiritual intelligence: What we can learn from the early awakening child.* Maryknoll, NY: Orbis Books.

Sisk, D., & Torrance, E. P. (2001). *Spiritual intelligence: Developing higher consciousness.* Buffalo, NY: Creative Education Foundation Press.

Sriraman, B. (2009). Spirituality. In B. Kerr (Ed.), *Encyclopedia of giftedness, creativity, and talent* (pp. 823-824). Thousand Oaks, CA: Sage Publications.

Sternberg, R. J. (1988). Three-facet model of creativity. In R. J. Sternberg (Ed.), *The nature of creativity: Contemporary psychological perspectives.* (pp. 125-147). New York, NY: Cambridge University Press.

Torrance, E. P. (1995). *Why fly?* Norwood, NJ: Ablex Publishing Corporation.

Vaughan, F. (1979). *Awakening intuition.* New York, NY: Anchor Press.

Vaughan, F. (2002). What is spiritual intelligence? *Journal of Humanistic Psychology, 42*(2), 16-33.

Wigglesworth, C. (2012). *SQ21: The twenty-one skills of spiritual intelligence.* New York, NY: Select Books.

Zohar, D., & Marshall, I. (2000). *SQ: Connecting with our spiritual intelligence.* New York, NY: Bloomsbury Publishing.

Zohar, D., & Marshall, I. (2004). *Spiritual capital: Wealth we can live by.* San Francisco, CA: Berrett-Koehler Publishers.

About the Author

Rebecca DiLiberto earned an M.S. in Creativity from the International Center for Studies in Creativity at SUNY Buffalo State, and a B.A. in Art/Design, with a Minor in Computer Applications from SUNY Cortland. Rebecca ascribes to the philosophy "you do not have to be unique to be creative; rather we are all uniquely creative." This philosophy guides her in cultivating the principles of creativity and proactively inspiring different ways of thinking to promote meaningful change in herself and others. Rebecca's ultimate vision is to foster personal growth and creativity in others, to lead them toward a more purposeful life and greater well-being.

Email: AllUniquelyCreative@gmail.com

SOCIAL CAPITAL &
CREATIVITY

Does Culture Affect Creativity?
An Integrative Literature Review

Mattia Miani
International Center for Studies in Creativity
SUNY Buffalo State

Abstract

This paper presents an integrative literature review of the study of cross-cultural issues in creativity. It analyzes five areas: conceptions of creativity across cultures, effect of culture on creativity production, effect of multicultural experience on individual levels of creativity, validity of creativity methods across cultures, and the relationship between studies in creativity and studies in differences in thinking patterns across cultures. For each of these areas, the paper offers a view of the questions that remain unanswered in the literature and makes recommendation for further research. "Does culture affect creativity?" is the overarching question this paper attempts to answer. The conclusion is that the construct of culture is very important in illuminating creativity in a global perspective, but, at the same time, it may conceal other forces that shape the different forms that creativity takes around the world.

Does Culture Affect Creativity?
An Integrative Literature Review

Phenomena such as the globalization of business, the international mobility of the highly-skilled workforce, and the multiplication of social and economic exchanges made possible by the new media, make the introduction of a cross-cultural perspective in the study of creativity particularly important (Westwood & Low, 2003; Zhao, 2012).

This paper presents an integrative literature review of studies on cross-cultural issues in creativity to answer the broader question of whether culture affects creativity. According to Torraco (2005), "the integrative literature review is a form of research that reviews, critiques, and synthesizes representative literature on a topic in an integrated way such that new frameworks and perspectives on the topic are generated" (p. 356).

This paper first presents how the review was conducted, and what was and was not included. Second, it presents how the topic was structured in previous reviews published in journals and handbooks. Third, it presents a sample of the literature available today in a number of key areas, in part already addressed in previous reviews and in part neglected. This will ultimately lead to answering the question about the relationship between culture and creativity.

How This Review Was Conducted

This review considers *creativity* to be a general mental and social process (Sawyer, 2006; Torrance, 1979). As a consequence, scholarly works on the creative industries and domain specific creative manifestations (e.g., fine arts) were excluded.

The term *cross-cultural* in this paper takes on two meanings: it refers to comparative studies of creativity in different cultures, and also refers to studies that focus on creativity in cultures different from North America and Western Europe. The assumption being made is that the academic literature on creativity, at least in English-speaking publications, has a perspective dominated by studies conducted in English speaking countries and universities based in Western Europe.

With these limits in mind, the work began by searching the indices of major creativity journals: *Journal of Creative Behavior, Creativity Research Journal, Thinking Skills and Creativity, Creativity and Innovation Management,* and *International Journal of Creativity and Problem Solving.*

Many more articles were found scattered among a variety of journals ranging from management to philosophy, found using targeted keyword searches on the online databases of SUNY Buffalo State and RMIT University. The keywords "multicultural," "culture," and "cross-cultural" were used in conjunction with "creativity" and "creative." Further documents, in particular a few books and proceedings, were identified using a "snowball" approach, by identifying new sources mentioned in the bibliographies of works under examination. Also added were references to books on creativity methods developed by authors outside North America and Western Europe.

The result was an extensive collection of around 70 references. Most came from literature published over the past 20 years, clearly showing a growing interest in the subject. This review does not present findings from all literature identified, but does focus on what the author considered to be the most representative pieces of research.

Previous Literature Reviews on Cross-Cultural Issues and Creativity

A number of reviews of this topic were published between 1990 and 2010. Niu and Sternberg (2002) developed a review comparing both implicit and explicit theories of creativity across cultures. Their conclusion is that people in different countries have similar, but not identical views of what creativity is (essentially agreeing with the results of Rudowicz & Hui, 1997). In particular, people living in the Far East tend to associate creativity more with moral and social values while people living in the West tend to associate the concept of creativity more with individual accomplishments. When it comes to testing explicit theories of creativity, the authors showed skepticism in employing divergent thinking tests across cultures (including the Torrance Tests of Creative Thinking; Torrance, 1966), since they are based on a specific view of creativity, and suggested that more meaningful results might be achieved using product-oriented tasks and consensual measurement. From this point of view, the plethora of studies that seem to favor the Westerner in divergent thinking tests may not be more significant than standardized IQ tests administered to people not familiar with the Western educational system and testing.

Westwood and Low (2003) analyzed different conceptions of creativity across cultures; social structural factors that may relate to creativity and innovation (e.g., the educational or religious systems); creativity as an aspect of cognition and personality; and the relationship between creativity and cultural values. Overall, the authors downplayed the role of cultural differences, contending that the literature on cultural values leads to oversimplified, one-dimensional comparisons (e.g., individualistic vs. collectivist societies), and emphasized the social and institutional factors (e.g., the educational system) that can affect how creativity is valued and practiced in a society.

Lubart (1990, 2010) has paid much attention to the phenomenon and has written a number of extensive reviews. In an early work, Lubart (1990) focused on the effect of cultural environments on creativity, addressing four topics from a cross-cultural perspective: definitions of creativity, the creative process, the direction in which creativity is channeled, and the degree to which creativity is nurtured. Later, Lubart (2010) structured the relationship between culture—mostly national culture—and creativity in three main areas of inquiry: conceptions of culture across cultures, relationship between culture and amount of creativity expressed, and the effects of multicultural experiences (e.g., living abroad) on creativity.

Conceptions of Creativity

Niu and Sternberg (2002) asked, "Is there a truly global concept of creativity?" (p. 270). The answer that emerges from the literature is both a qualified "yes" and a qualified "no." The dimension of novelty seems to be associated with the concept of creativity almost universally (Lubart, 2010). The disagreements begin emerging when further qualifications of the concept (e.g., usefulness of the new idea) come into play.

Lubart (1990) claimed that Western definitions are prominently product-oriented, while in Eastern definitions it is impossible to separate the product and the individual. For example, in Hinduism creativity is seen more as a psychic state than as a process or product. Lubart further explained that sometimes creativity can be accepted in a well-defined niche (e.g., dance for the Samoan people studied by Margaret Mead), but the same culture can actually squelch creative practices in other areas (e.g., education for the Samoans).

One interesting commonality across cultures is what can be called the "doublespeak" about creativity. Many countries and societies praise creativity, yet suppress and discourage creative contributions (Staw, 1996; Thompson, 2014). This tendency has been documented, for example, in the school setting. Dawson, D'Andrea, Affinito, and Westby (1999), citing previous research conducted mainly in North America, summarized that

> teachers tend to dislike children who display the characteristics of the creative personality.... On the other hand, this research might be

seen as quite surprising, given that teachers generally acknowledge the importance of creativity as an educational goal. (p. 58)

Similarly, Chan and Chan (1999) reported that characteristics normally associated with creative individuals (e.g., nonconformity and expressiveness) are disliked by Chinese teachers in their pupils. Nearly identical conclusions were drawn studying Korean students and teachers (Lim & Plucker, 2001).

Even the way in which the concept of creativity itself is framed in a study is subject to the cultural bias of the researcher. For this reason, it is refreshing that there is increasing interest in studying creativity among Asian scholars (as shown by Lau, Hiu, & Ng, 2004; Ng, 2001, 2004; Singh 2004; Sinha 2008).

It may remain difficult to disentangle the conflicting views on creativity in a specific context because of the hybrid nature of globalized culture and multiple influences that exercise their power on individuals working in transnational and multicultural environments. However, at least to some extent, cultural orientations seem to affect the perception and definition of creativity.

Creativity and National Cultures

It has become almost a commonplace to state that individuals in the West (English speaking countries and Western Europe) are more creative than individuals in the East (China and Confucian heritage societies). A Singaporean scholar educated in Australia, Ng (2001), showed that Asian societies squelch individual creativity more than Western societies. Ng (2001) described two ideal types of individuals struggling between creativity and conformity:

By yielding their personal autonomy to the social group in this way, they gain its approval, as well as preserve its internal unity and harmony. However, conducting themselves in this restrained and somewhat self-deprecating manner will limit their capacity for creative / critical thinking.

This is in marked contrast to the non-conforming and group-independent individuals, who show a psychological need for autonomy, independence and separation from the social group.... By behaving this carefree and self-gratifying manner, they risk the censure of the group, as well as threaten its internal unity and harmony. However, maintaining their personal autonomy from the group enables these individuals to engage in creative / critical thinking. (p. 56)

Needless to say, according to Ng, Asians tend to fall into the first ideal type, Westerners into the second. Ng is hardly the first scholar to note these differences. Weber (1915/1951) was perhaps the first to identify this difference between East and West when he analyzed the religions of China. He claimed that the social conservatism of the Chinese stemmed from their valuing status over performance and achievement. Many scholars link the lack of individual creativity in Confucian heritage societies to the Confucian values of conformity and obedience (Kim, 2007; Lubart & Sternberg, 1998; Weiner, 2000).

However, establishing such one-dimensional causal connections between two very complex constructs such as creativity and culture may be misleading. In some cases, these differences may not be due to cultural factors per se, but may be related to other social and economic factors. Mar'I and Karayanni (1983), reviewing two decades of research, noted that while Westerners seem to score better than individuals from the Middle East in divergent thinking tests, actually the same differences may be found among individuals of Arabic culture when comparing subjects who are more or less modernized. This suggests that modernization factors (e.g., freedom of expression, access to a variety of media, higher disposable income, time for leisure) can be the real differentiating factor behind divergent thinking scores.

History tends to confirm this view; depending on the chosen chronological point, the same country or region can show a great deal of creativity, or not. One example is Japan, which used to be seen as a country of imitators, but in the 1980s became highly regarded for its creative outputs in industry, design, and popular culture (Tatsuno, 1989).

One final example will prove the difficulty in making causal statements when it comes to connecting culture and creativity. Lubart (2010) suggested that "collectivist values may foster, via processes involving compromise, incremental innovations (as opposed to radical innovations), with people working together toward creativity in a collective interest" (p. 274). A surface reading of this statement could lead one to claim that collectivist societies prefer incremental creativity and individualistic societies favor radical innovation. Is it true? Let's take Japan, a society that unquestionably falls at the high end of the collectivist scale, and test the hypothesis on a random domain: fountain pens (Gerosa, 2012; Lambrou & Sunami, 2012). Japanese craftsmen are known for applying the millenary arts of urushi (a type of lacquer) and maki-e (a type of painting on lacquer) to fountain pens. They have been perfecting this specific application since the 1930s when Namiki pens were chosen by Dunhill, of London, for export into the Western markets. But if you look closer, you can easily find a number of breakthrough innovations coming from Japan: in 1963 engineers at Pilot invented a fountain pen with a retractable nib that remains in production today, and is regarded as a design icon (sometimes referred to as "capless" or "vanishing point"). Another pen company, Platinum, has recently introduced the "slip and seal" mechanism to cap its fountain pens in a hermetic way, thus preventing the ink from drying for an unprecedented length of time. Sailor has pioneered the use of unusual materials to build groundbreaking fountain pens, including amber, ceramics, and susutake (a type of bamboo), and has introduced a series of never-seen-before nibs. In summary, when it comes to fountain pens, Japanese industries and craftsmen can be either incremental or radical innovators; one does not exclude the other. This simple sketch cannot be used to formulate a general rule, but is enough to disprove the initial generalization, and shows how difficult it is to establish causal connections between culture and creativity in its various dimensions (including its extension in innovation processes).

Cross-cultural Experience and Creativity

The literature on the effect of multicultural exposure on individual levels of creativity would support a separate review; this paper will rely on a few exemplary studies.

Maddux and Galinsky (2009) found that Western students who spent time overseas were more likely to come up with innovative insights upon their return. Fee and Gray (2012) tested the hypothesis of a link between creativity and expatriate experience in a longitudinal study. They measured changes in the creative-thinking abilities of a sample of expatriates over the first 12 months of their placement. When compared with a control group of non-expatriates, the expatriates showed significant increases in overall creative-thinking abilities and cognitive flexibility, although not originality, elaboration, or ideational fluency (Fee & Gray, 2012).

These studies are quite typical as they measure the impact of time spent abroad. However, the time spent abroad itself may not be the direct variable influencing gains in creativity. In a contiguous field, cross-cultural competence, it has been demonstrated that only "reflective" cultural experiences abroad will have lasting effects on one's cross-cultural competence; this means that students abroad or expats hanging out with other individuals from their home country will not be particularly affected (Hammer, 2012, p. 126). The same could apply to gains in creativity.

Chua (2011) contributed an interesting perspective: what counts is not living abroad, but developing multicultural professional networks. However, his findings are limited to tasks that require cross-cultural knowledge.

Certainly more research is needed in this area, taking into account that multi-cultural exposure may now take many forms, such as working in a multicultural team or organization, virtually connecting with people living abroad for leisure or business, and adopting fashions and ideas originated in another cultural context.

Creativity Methods in Cross-Cultural Perspective

One area of inquiry that has received limited attention so far is the effectiveness of creativity methods across cultures. Lubart (1990), one of the few authors to mention the problem, quoted only three studies; and of these, only one suggested alternatives to the classic four-stage process (Wallas, 1926).

Some research on the cross-cultural effectiveness of the Osborn-Parnes Creative Problem Solving (CPS) process exists. (For a history of CPS, see Puccio, Murdock, & Mance, 2005). In a very early study, Lindgren and Lindgren (1965) used individual-group-individual brainstorming, and assessed its effects on ideation and originality in a group of art students from the Middle East in Beirut. By comparing the outcomes with a previous study conducted with students in San Francisco, they concluded that "the method may be considered to have been even more successful with the Middle East subjects, inasmuch as gains in number of responses were achieved by both sexes in the experimental group" (Lindgren & Lindgren, 1965, p. 26). They also warned that results may not be replicable in languages different than English since other languages may lack the same level of directedness.

Puccio & González (2004), discussing creativity issues in the East, claimed that "practices that have been developed for nurturing creative thinking in the West, and primarily in the United States, [can] be directly applied to audiences in the East" (p. 407). This idea is shared by many CPS facilitators who have worked with organizations in Asia (B. Miller, personal communication, October 3, 2013).

Some research seems to support this position. Basadur, Wakabayashi, and Takai (1992) measured divergent thinking attitudes in a group of Japanese managers before and after training in CPS. The experimental group of 60 people showed significant gains on these measures versus two control groups. Compared to North American managers from similar studies, the Japanese managers appeared to make at least equal gains after training. Later on, Basadur, Pringle, and Kirkland (2002) used the same research design with a group of South American managers, with the group again showing significant gains in divergent thinking measures. This led the authors to conclude that "the concepts and methods of similar training provided in previous Japanese and North American research are applicable to Spanish-speaking South American managers" (Basadur et al., 2002, p. 395), and hinted at broader applicability if replicated in other countries.

Other research questions that have been neglected so far have to do with the cultural origin of these methods. Are creativity methods a domain of North American and European thinkers? It is fairly easy to answer no. However, in many cases, for many decades, researchers in the West did not have access to foreign creative-thinking methodologies due to political and linguistic barriers. For example, it is not an accident that TRIZ methodology (Altshuller, 1999) became popular outside its home country, Azerbaijan, and the states of the former Soviet Union, only after the fall of the iron curtain. Another example is the K-J Method, which originated in Japan in the 1960s (Kawakita, 1991) and was first mentioned in the West by Torrance (1979), but remained inaccessible until recent times when articles and training courses in English appeared outside Japan (Kunifuji, 2013; Nomura, 2013; Scupin, 1997).

The questions that remain to be answered are whether these methods differ in any significant way and whether the differences may be explained by cultural factors. At first glance, similarities seem to outmatch differences, such that a synthesis is possible (Sawyer, 2013). For example, in many of these methods it is possible to find rounds of divergent and convergent thinking, clustering, and transformative processes (Nomura, 2013).

The social and cultural context seems to clearly influence at least some of these methods. For example, Radjou, Prabhu and Ahuja (2012) popularized the term "Jugaad" to indicate frugal innovation. Jugaad is a Hindu term that indicates an ingenious fix derived from a very limited pool of resources. While the concept is clearly situated in the reality of a developing country, the concepts of Jugaad have been embraced by major corporations worldwide on a mission to solve engineering problems in more cost-effective ways.

Creativity and Thinking

One area of inquiry that is relatively untouched is the relationship between creativity and culturally-influenced modes of thinking.

Research supports the view that cognitive differences are the deepest and most challenging sources of misunderstanding and conflict in cross-cultural groups (Shweder, 1991). Nisbett (2003) came to conceptualize a "geography of thought" in which remarkable differences between Westerners (North Americans, in his studies) and Asians (Chinese, Japanese, and Koreans) could be found in an impressive number of experiments on attention, perception, and cognition. Kase,

Slocum, and Zhang (2011) applied this line of inquiry to the field of managerial cognition and found major differences in the thinking models applied by Western and Eastern managers. In brief, what they found was that Asian managers were more inductive in their thinking, while American and European managers were more likely to adopt a deductive thinking pattern (Kase et al., 2011).

Arguably, this research can be useful for creativity scholars. Rather than using complex and indistinct constructs such as *Confucianism* or *Western culture*, this literature provides evidence of differences in basic mental operations that can more easily be related to creative thinking patterns.

Conclusions

Cross-cultural issues in the study of creativity have become increasingly part of the research agenda of scholars in the field. As this paper has shown, the past 20 years have witnessed an increasing number of studies and an increasing cultural diversity in the authorship of these studies. So, is there a causal link between culture and creativity? Research has established a few interim conclusions that seem to support, at least to some extent, certain effects of culture upon creativity: conceptions of culture may subtly vary across cultures; different institutional settings may, to a certain extent, foster or squelch creativity; and exposure to cross-cultural experiences may increase the level of individual creativity, at least under certain circumstances.

These conclusions, however, can be seen only as interim achievements, since research is still dominated by a number of simplified assumptions about the relationship between culture and creativity. Much of the time culture is examined only at the national level, where it is a much more complex construct. Many areas of inquiry remain open for researchers. More research on the cross-cultural validity of creativity methods would be useful, given that many of these methods will likely be used in today's increasingly-common multicultural groups and international businesses. Further, studies on cross-cultural variations in basic psychological processes can offer creativity scholars very useful benchmarks for advancing a research agenda on the cross-cultural nature of creative thinking.

While studying the connection between creativity and culture seems to mean dealing with sometimes-muddy concepts, it is still a rewarding exercise since it can help us to improve mutual understanding between diverse groups and achieve breakthrough results when working across cultures or in multicultural teams. While it may not be possible to answer the initial question in a definitive way at this time, focused studies will help us better understand where and how culture and creativity are interrelated and affect each other.

References

Altshuller, G. (1999). *The innovation algorithm: TRIZ, systematic innovation, and technical creativity*. Worcester, MA: Technical Innovation Center.

Basadur, M., Pringle, P., & Kirkland, D. (2002). Crossing cultures: Training effects on the divergent thinking attitudes of Spanish-speaking South American managers. *Creativity Research Journal, 14*(3-4), 395-408.

Basadur, M., Wakabayashi, M., & Takai, J. (1992). Training effects on the divergent thinking attitudes of Japanese managers. *International Journal of Intercultural Relations, 16*(3), 329-345.

Chan, D., & Chan, L. K. (1999). Implicit theories of creativity: Teachers' perception of student characteristics in Hong Kong. *Creativity Research Journal, 12*(3), 185-195.

Chua, R. Y. J. (2011). *Innovating at the world's crossroads: How multicultural networks promote creativity* (Working Paper No. 11-085). Retrieved from Harvard Business School: http://www.hbs.edu/faculty/Publication%20 Files/11-085.pdf

Dawson, V. L., D'Andrea, T., Affinito, R., & Westby, E. L. (1999). Predicting creative behavior: A reexamination of the divergence between traditional and teacher-defined concepts of creativity. *Creativity Research Journal, 12*(1), 57-66.

Fee, A., & Gray, J. S. (2012). The expatriate-creativity hypothesis: A longitudinal field test. *Human Relations, 65*(12), 1515-1538.

Gerosa, A. (2012). *Maki-e: A story waiting to be written*. Milan, Italy: Ops.

Hammer, M. (2012). The Intercultural Development Inventory: A new frontier in assessment and development of intercultural competence. In M. Vande Berg, R. M. Paige, & K. H. Lou (Eds.), *Student Learning Abroad* (pp. 115-136). Sterling, VA: Stylus Publishing.

Kase, K., Slocum, A., & Zhang, Y. (2011). *Asian versus Western management thinking: Its culture-bound nature*. New York, NY: Palgrave Macmillan.

Kawakita, J. (1991) *The original KJ method* (rev. ed.). Meguro, Tokyo: Kawakita Research Institute.

Kim, K. H. (2007). Exploring the interactions between Asian culture (Confucianism) and creativity. *Journal of Creative Behavior, 41*(1), 28-53.

Kunifuji, S. (2013). A Japanese problem solving approach: the KJ Ho Method. In A. M. J. Skulimowski & J. Kacprzyk (Eds.), *Proceedings of the 8th International Conference on Knowledge, Information and Creativity*

Support Systems (pp. 333-338). Kraków, Poland: Progress & Business Publishers.

Lambrou, A., & Sunami, M. (2012). *Fountain pens of Japan*. El Paso, TX: Andreas Lambrou Publishers Limited.

Lau, S., Hiu, A., & Ng, G. (Eds.) (2004). *Creativity. When East meets West*. Singapore: World Scientific Publishing.

Lim, W., & Plucker, J. A. (2001). Creativity through a lens of social responsibility: Implicit theories of creativity with Korean samples. *Journal of Creative Behavior, 35*(2), 115-130.

Lindgren, H. C., & Lindgren, F. (1965). Creativity, brainstorming, and orneriness: A cross-cultural study. *The Journal of Social Psychology, 67*, 23-30.

Lubart, T. I. (1990). Creativity and cross-cultural variation. *International Journal of Psychology, 25*, 39-59.

Lubart, T. I. (2010). Cross-cultural perspectives on creativity. In J. C. Kaufman & R. J. Sternberg (Eds.), *The Cambridge handbook of creativity* (pp. 265-278). New York, NY: Cambridge University Press.

Lubart, T. I., & Sternberg, R. J. (1998). Creativity across time and place: Life span and cross-cultural perspectives. *High Ability Studies, 9*(1), 59-74.

Maddux, W. W., & Galinsky, A. D. (2009). Cultural borders and mental barriers: The relationship between living abroad and creativity. *Journal of Personality and Social Psychology, 96*(5), 1047-1061.

Mar'I, S. K., & Karayanni, M. (1983). Creativity in Arab culture: Two decades of research. *Journal of Creative Behavior, 16*(4), 227-238.

Ng, A. K. (2001). *Why Asians are less creative than Westerners*. Singapore: Prentice Hall.

Ng, A. K. (2004). *Liberating the creative spirit in Asian students*. Singapore: Prentice Hall.

Nisbett, R. E. (2003). *The geography of thought*. New York, NY: Free Press.

Niu, W. H., & Sternberg, R. J. (2002). Contemporary studies on the concept of creativity: The East and the West. *The Journal of Creative Behavior, 36*(4), 269-288.

Nomura, T. (2013). Introduction to KJ-Ho: A Japanese problem solving approach. *Creativity & Human Development*. Retrieved from www.creativityjournal.net/index.php/contents/articles/item/201-kj-ho_japanese_problem_solving

Puccio, G. J., & González, D. W. (2004). Nurturing creative thinking. Western approaches and Eastern issues. In S. Lau, A. Hiu, & G. Ng (Eds.), *Creativity: When East meets West* (pp. 393-426). Singapore: World Scientific Publishing.

Puccio, G. J., Murdock, M. C., & Mance, M. (2005). Current developments in creative problem solving for organizations: A focus on thinking skills and styles. *Korean Journal of Thinking and Problem Solving, 15*(2), 43-76.

Radjou, N., Prabhu, J., & Ahuja, S. (2012). *Jugaad innovation: A frugal and flexible approach to innovation for the 21st century.* New Delhi, India: Random House India.

Rudowicz, E., & Hui, A. (1997). The creative personality: Hong Kong perspective. *Journal of Social Behavior & Personality, 12*(1), 139-157.

Sawyer, K. (2013). *Zig zag: The surprising path to greater creativity.* San Francisco, CA: Jossey-Bass.

Sawyer, R. K. (2006). *Explaining creativity: The science of human innovation.* New York, NY: Oxford University Press.

Scupin, R. (1997). The KJ method: A technique for analyzing data derived from Japanese ethnology. *Human Organization, 56*(2), 233-237.

Shweder, R. (1991). *Thinking through cultures.* Cambridge, MA: Harvard University Press.

Singh, K. (2004). *Thinking hats and coloured turbans: Creativity across cultures.* Singapore: Prentice Hall.

Sinha, K. (2008). *China's creative imperative: How creativity is transforming society and business in China.* Hoboken, NJ: Wiley.

Staw, B. M. (1996). Why no one really wants creativity. In C. M. Ford & D. A. Gioia (Eds.), *Creative action in organizations: Ivory tower visions and real world voices.* Thousand Oaks, CA: Sage Publications.

Tatsuno, S. M. (1989). *Created in Japan. From imitators to world-class innovators.* New York, NY: Ballinger.

Thompson, D. (2014, October 10). *Why experts reject creativity.* Retrieved from http://www.theatlantic.com/business/archive/2014/10/why-new-ideas-fail/381275

Torraco, R. J. (2005). Writing integrative literature reviews: Guidelines and examples. *Human Resource Development Review, 4*(3), 356-367.

Torrance, E. P. (1966). *Torrance Tests of Creative Thinking: Norms-technical manual research edition—Verbal Tests, Forms A and B—Figural Tests, Forms A and B.* Princeton, NJ: Personnel Press.

Torrance, E. P. (1979). *The search for satori and creativity*. Buffalo, NY: Creative Education Foundation.

Wallas, G. (1926). *The art of thought*. New York, NY: Harcourt, Brace & Company.

Weber, M. (1951). *The religion of China* (H. H. Gerth, Ed. and Trans.). Glencoe, IL: Free Press. (Original work published in German in 1915).

Weiner, R. P. (2000). *Creativity and beyond: Cultures, values and change*. Albany, NY: State University of New York Press.

Westwood, R., & Low, D. R. (2003). The multicultural muse: Culture, creativity and innovation. *International Journal of Cross Cultural Management, 3*(2), 235-259.

Zhao, Y. (2012). *World class learners: Educating creative and entrepreneurial students*. Thousand Oaks, CA: Corwin.

About the Author

Mattia Miani is based in Vietnam where he designs, develops, and delivers learning programs for industry and government with a focus on creativity and leadership. He holds a degree in Communication Sciences and an EMBA from the University of Bologna (Italy) and a Master of Science in Creativity from SUNY Buffalo State.

Mattia is a certified trainer, instructional designer, and lecturer, having achieved an Australian Graduate Certificate in Tertiary Teaching and Learning, an American Graduate Certificate in Instructional Design, an Australian Diploma of Training Design and Development, and an Australian Certificate IV in Training and Assessment. He has logged more than 4,000 hours of teaching at all levels: executive, postgraduate, undergraduate, and vocational.

For his work in Vietnam in 2014 he received the Firestien Family Creative Achievement Award from the International Center for Studies of Creativity.

Email: mattiainasia@gmail.com

Do Teachers Value Creativity?

Serap Gurak Ozdemir
International Center for Studies in Creativity
SUNY Buffalo State

Abstract

Most teachers have misconceptions about creativity (Kampylis, 2010). They may think creativity is related to gifted students, or they link creativity solely with the arts (Craft, 2003; Fryer, 1996; Kampylis, 2010). Therefore, they may underestimate the creative potential of all students (Esquivel, 1995). Yet, teachers are critical factors for developing creativity in their students. Creativity training could help teachers to understand creative students and to encourage creativity in the classroom. This paper summarizes common beliefs about creativity in education, reviews teacher perspectives and creative student characteristics, and discusses the importance of teacher training on creativity to enhance effectiveness of teaching in the classroom.

Do Teachers Value Creativity?

Friend: I heard that you are going to teach in a village.

Serap: Yes, I will! I am very excited. This is going to be my first teaching experience.

Friend: Honey, let me tell you this. That is going to be very hard. I have been teaching these students more than 10 years. They just do not get it.

Serap: Maybe I can teach them. I believe I can make a difference.

Friend: Hahaha, I know. This is your first experience, and you are excited. But you will see what I am talking about!

This is how my career began, as a teacher of 7th grade science in the village of Burdur, Turkey. The classroom was an inclusive general education classroom. More than half of my students were diagnosed with a learning disability, Attention Deficit Disorder, or emotional and behavioral disorders, possibly caused by consanguineous marriages. In addition to significant behavioral issues, the students had limited knowledge about science subjects. It was disheartening. After my first day of school, I was talking to myself and repeating again and again that my friend couldn't be right. I decided that I was going to fight.

One of my biggest challenges was a student, Demir, who was extremely disruptive, non-conformist, and disturbing to his peers. It was very hard for him to focus and pay attention during instruction, and he used humor in an unproductive way. When I asked other teachers about Demir, I heard only negative attitudes and comments. None of teachers believed him capable of being a successful student. Even though their comments were convincing, one of my lessons changed everything.

The lesson was about the excretory system. During the lesson, Demir was not interested in the topic; he contributed to the lesson by making a joke: "We all are familiar with this system because we use the restrooms every day." I was upset about the joke and told him to prepare an assignment that would show how this system works. When he asked how many paragraphs he needed to write, I said to use his creativity and to do whatever he wanted. Then I gave him a nudge: I knew that he was very interested in rap music, so I directed him to use his interests. The next class when talking about the excretory system, he was very excited and interested in the class. He had prepared a rap and sang it in the class. This was the beginning of a very productive and joyful semester for him and the rest of the class.

After teaching one year in this school, I came to the United States. One day, I received an email from a former colleague in Burdur about my students there. The email described the successes my students were experiencing. In Turkey, students take a national exam at the end of the 8th grade before proceeding on to high school. In this exam, after having one school year with me, my students scored an average of 11 out of 20 in science, while scoring an average of 4 out of 20 in other core subjects. The administrator wanted to find out *what I had done differently.*

Now, after studying creativity for the last two years, I can clearly answer that the thing I did differently was to bring creativity into my classroom. However, this question led to other questions about the connections between creativity and teachers. *What does a teacher think about creativity? What are their perceptions about creativity characteristics? What could be the benefits of creativity training for teachers?*

Teachers' Misconceptions of Creativity

There are a number of misconceptions teachers have about creativity. First, some teachers believe that creativity is a rare trait in education (Fryer & Collings, 1991). More specifically, a common conception of creativity is that it is a trait only of gifted students (Kampylis, 2010). Teachers who believe this may underestimate the potential of all students (Esquivel, 1995), a view which severely limits the spread of creativity in education. Alternately, there is widespread belief that every student is creative and can be successful in his/her own way (Fryer, 1996; Renzulli & Reis, 2009). Creativity needs to be nurtured in education as a life skill in fast-changing world in which future is unpredictable (Puccio, Mance, Barbero Switalski, & Reali, 2012; Trilling & Fadel, 2012).

Second, some teachers believe that creativity is only linked with the arts (Craft, 2003; Fryer, 1996; Kampylis, 2010). This misunderstanding is a symptom of *art bias,* a viewpoint which says that creativity is a characteristic only of individuals with artistic talent (Runco, 2007). Therefore, teachers may believe that creativity is inappropriate for core subjects such as science or mathematics (Cropley, 1990). This belief represents a gap between the implicit perspectives of teachers and explicit theories of creativity, which suggest embedding creativity in all subject areas and fostering creative learning by all teachers (Kampylis, 2010; Starko, 2014).

The third misconception about creativity in the classroom is a mismatch between what teachers say they value in terms of creativity, and what they say they value in terms of ideal student characteristics. Broadly stated, teachers valued creativity in the classrooms, but not students' creative behaviors (Runco & Johnson, 2002; Scott, 1999; Westby & Dawson, 1995).

In traditional classroom settings, students are educated to fit a particular description of "ideal" student (Murphy, 1984; Torrance, 1963, 1975), and unfortunately, most "ideal student" traits do not overlap with creative students' traits (Dettmer, 1981; Scott, 1999; Torrance, 1963, 1975; Westby & Dawson, 1995). Therefore, teachers could perceive creative characteristics as being hard to manage in their classrooms (Fletcher, 2011). For instance, teachers consider *conformity* to be one of the most important traits for the ideal student (Bachtold, 1974; Kaltsounis, 1978; Torrance, 1965). Conformity was also ranked first on the Ideal Child Checklist by both teachers and parents (Torrance, 1963). Accordingly, *lack of conformity,* which is one of the characteristics of creative individuals, may create a challenge for creative students and for their teachers.

Guncer and Oral (1993) conducted a correlational study to understand teachers' perceptions of creative students in terms of conformity. The Torrance Tests of Creative Thinking (TTCT) were used to evaluate student creativity. The Teacher Perception Scale was used to determine teacher perceptions of students in terms of conformity to school discipline. The results of this study indicated that conformity was negatively correlated with creativity, based on teacher rankings of creative students. Teachers in the study described creative students as nonconformist and disruptive. Dawson (1997) also concluded that creative students were seen as trouble by their teachers. Similarly, Scott (1999) explored teachers' biases toward creative children by comparing teachers' rankings with undergraduate students' rankings on the Scott Teacher Perception Scale. One of the findings was that creative students were found to be more disruptive and harder to control in the classroom. Additionally, teachers emphasized that these students were the least-favorite students in their classrooms.

As with the studies on conformity, other studies of creative students showed a bias against traits exhibited by creative students. For instance, studies have shown that creative students were eager to think divergently and to demonstrate these characteristics, while these same behaviors were perceived as disruptive by teachers (Guncer & Oral, 1993; Scott, 1999; Torrance, 1963). A study of sixth graders suggested that the gap might be partially based in perception or expectations: Williams, Poole, and Lett (1979) found that creative students, despite their reputations, did value teacher-desired qualities such as diligence, obedience, cooperation, and attentiveness, but that teachers may discount these traits when they appear in creative children.

In my school in Burdur, Turkey, these misconceptions were on vivid display. My teacher friend (the one who had said the students there "just do not get it") could not have seen creativity in her classroom even if the potential was there. In her mind creativity was a characteristic of giftedness, and she did not believe that any of the students there could be academically gifted. In a similar way, I was subject to misconceptions, too, because I had not yet learned about the many aspects of creativity. With my student Demir, my goal was simply to stop his destructive behavior and make him into my version of an "ideal" student. I tapped into his creativity inadvertently.

There is some evidence that these impressions might be changing, or that they are not held everywhere. Aljughaiman and Mowrer-Reynolds (2005) used seven closed-ended and seven open-ended statements to understand teachers' beliefs on creativity in the classroom, and to rate characteristics of creative students. Surprisingly, compared to previous studies (Westby & Dawson, 1995), teachers did not rank negative characteristics, such as disruptive and nonconformist, first. The first five characteristics of creative students were *thinks differently, imaginative, artistic, has rich vocabulary,* and *intelligent.* Further, more than fifty percent of teachers in the study answered that creativity *can* be taught to anyone and *can* be improved in the classroom.

A recent study conducted by Gurak-Ozdemir (2016) investigated teachers' perceptions of creative students in terms of their cognitive styles. This study showed that teachers have a tendency to support characteristics associated with their own cognitive styles. The findings emphasized that there was no one ideal student description, but that it depends on how teachers perceive them in terms of their differences.

As teachers, we not only have misconceptions about creativity, but also about student behavior overall. In Burdur's classrooms, Demir was non-conformist, disruptive, intelligent, artistic, and a different thinker. It was easy for teachers to tag him as troublemaker, but I believe that teachers have a responsibility to understand students' individual differences and provide them with learning environments that suit their differences. All of this suggests that teacher training for creativity would help teachers to understand different student characteristics and how to make use of these characteristics in a positive way.

Diakidoy, I. A. N., & Kanari, E. (1999). Student teachers' beliefs about creativity. *British Educational Research Journal, 25,* 225-243.

Esquivel, G. B. (1995). Teacher behaviors that foster creativity. *Educational Psychology Review, 7,* 185-201.

Fletcher, L. S. (2011). Creative thinking in schools: Finding the "just right" challenge for students. *Gifted Child Today, 34,* 37-42.

Fryer, M. (1996). *Creative teaching and learning.* London, UK: Paul Chapman Publishing Ltd.

Fryer, M., & Collings, J. A. (1991). British teachers' views of creativity. *Journal of Creative Behavior, 25,* 75-81.

Guncer, B., & Oral, G. (1993). Relationship between creativity and nonconformity to school discipline as perceived by teachers of Turkish elementary school children, by controlling for their grade and sex. *Journal of Instructional Psychology, 20,* 208-214.

Gurak-Ozdemir, S. (2016). *Teachers' perceptions of students' creativity characteristics.* [Unpublished Master's Thesis.] Retrieved from http://digitalcommons.buffalostate.edu/creativetheses/28/

Halpin, G., Goldenberg G, R., & Halpin, G. (1973). Are creative teachers more humanistic in their pupil control ideologies? *Journal of Creative Behavior, 7*(4), 282-286.

Hansen, J. B., & Feldhusen, J. F. (1994). Comparison of trained and untrained teachers of gifted students. *Gifted Child Quarterly, 38,* 115-123.

Kaltsounis, B. (1978). Creative performance among siblings of various ordinal birth positions. *Psychological Reports, 42,* 915-918.

Kampylis, P. G. (2010). Fostering creative thinking: The role of primary teachers. In S. Puuronen (Ed.), *Jyväskylä studies in computing 115* (pp. 19-136). Finland: University of Jyväskylä.

Lin, C. F., Yeh, Y. C., Hung, Y. H., & Chang, R. I. (2013). Data mining for providing a personalized learning path in creativity: An application of decision trees. *Computers & Education, 68,* 199-210.

McGreevy, A. (1990). Tracking the creative teacher. *Momentum, 21,* 57-59.

Mohan, M. (1973). Is there a need for a course in creativity in teacher education? *Journal of Creative Behavior, 7,* 175-186.

Murphy, D. (1984). A new criterion for the "ideal" child? *Gifted Child Quarterly, 28,* 31-36.

Puccio, G. J., Mance, M., Barbero Switalski, L., & Reali, P. D. (2012). *Creativity rising: Creative thinking and creative problem solving in the 21st century.* Buffalo, NY: ICSC Press.

Renzulli, J. S., & Reis, S. M. (2009). *Light up your child's mind: Finding a unique pathway to happiness and success.* New York, NY: Little, Brown.

Runco, M. (2007). *Creativity: Theories and themes: Research, development, and practice.* Burlington, MA: Elsevier Academic Press

Runco, M. A., & Johnson, D. J. (2002). Parents' and teachers' implicit theories of children's creativity: A cross-cultural perspective. *Creativity Research Journal, 14,* 427-43.

Scott, C. L. (1999). Teachers' biases toward creative children. *Creativity Research Journal, 12,* 321-328.

Starko, A. J. (2014). *Creativity in the classroom: Schools of curious delight* (5th ed.). New York, NY: Routledge.

Stein, M. I. (1974). *Stimulating creativity in individuals.* New York, NY: Academic Press.

Torrance, E. P. (1963). The creative personality and the ideal pupil. *Teachers College Record, 65,* 220-226.

Torrance, E. P. (1965). *Rewarding creative behavior.* Englewood Cliffs, NJ: Prentice Hall.

Torrance, E. P. (1966). *Torrance Tests of Creative Thinking: Norms-technical manual research edition—Verbal Tests, Forms A and B—Figural Tests, Forms A and B.* Princeton, NJ: Personnel Press.

Torrance, E. P. (1975). Assessing children, teachers, and parents against the ideal child criterion. *Gifted Child Quarterly, 19,* 130-139.

Treffinger, D. J., Ripple, R. E., & Dacey, J. S. (1968). Teachers' attitudes about creativity. *Journal of Creative Behavior, 2,* 242-248.

Trilling, B., & Fadel, C. (2012). *21st century skills: Learning for life in our times.* San Francisco, CA: Jossey-Bass.

Westby, E. L., & Dawson, V. L. (1995). Creativity: Asset or burden in the classroom? *Creativity Research Journal, 8,* 1-10.

Whitlock, M. S., & DuCette, J. P. (1989). Outstanding and average teachers of the gifted: A comparative study. *Gifted Child Quarterly, 33,* 15-21.

Williams, A. J., Poole, M. E., & Lett, W. R. (1979). Actual and ideal self-perceptions of creative students. *Perceptual and Motor Skills, 48*(3), 995-1001.

About the Author

Serap Gurak Ozdemir is a creativity researcher. She is passionate about creativity in education, and her vision is to spread creativity in education all around the world. She completed her B.S. in Science and Technology Teaching at Dokuz Eylul University, Turkey. She also received a teaching certificate for Teachers of English to Speakers of Other Languages (TESOL) and a certificate of photography. She recently earned a Master of Science in Creativity from the International Center for Studies in Creativity at SUNY Buffalo State. She conducted research as her Master's thesis to investigate teachers' perceptions of an ideal student in terms of their FourSight preferences.

Email: serabiko3@gmail.com
LinkedIn: www.linkedin.com/in/serap-gurak-ozdemir-8b9521a1

How Can Teaching Creative Thinking Increase the Social Capital of Our Aging Population?

Virginia L. Bernd
International Center for Studies in Creativity
SUNY Buffalo State

Abstract

The aging members of our population have unique social and psychological needs. This paper argues that we can increase the social capital of the aging through creativity, and examines four aspects of successful aging in relation to the teaching of creative thinking and problem solving. Beginning with research on the mature mind that establishes the older adult as capable of continuing creative activities, this paper then establishes relationships between creative thinking, personal and community well-being, productive aging, and the development of social capital. The focus of this examination is to study the impact of programs for elders that encourage social interaction, team-building, and problem solving.

How Can Teaching Creative Thinking Increase the Social Capital of our Aging Population?

As the sliding doors of the senior center closed behind me, the voices of members enjoying coffee with friends in the nearby café drew my attention. I waved a greeting and hurried down the hall to where my fellow facilitators were prepping a classroom. We had been anxiously anticipating this day, when a group of seniors who had already taken our Introduction to Creative Problem Solving (CPS) workshop would be returning to begin the Applied CPS workshop. Here, they would be given a real challenge to address, presented to them by a client, the director of a local non-profit. The participants began arriving, reconnecting, and making themselves comfortable. We welcomed them back and reviewed the role they would play as a "creative think tank" for this community non-profit. The client would provide them with an overview of the challenge facing the organization, along with background information about the organization, its structure, and how it currently works within the community. They, the participants, would then have time to review all of the materials and return the next day with questions for the client before beginning their work as generators of creative ideas and innovative solutions. Their excitement was palpable.

During the next two weeks, the group met several times, sharing their work with the client, having the client choose the ideas she saw as best responding to her challenge, and complimenting the resource group on their ideas and insights. The seniors beamed with appreciation. When the satisfied client left with several viable solutions, the creative thinkers expressed their pleasure at having their ideas valued. The fact that they could continue to work with the client through the implementation stage interested a few and impressed them all with the realization that this was not only an exercise in problem solving, but also an opportunity to effect a positive change in their community.

Kawachi, chair of the Department of Social and Behavioral Sciences at the Harvard School of Public Health, writing with his medical colleagues, described social capital as represented by "civic engagement in local associations and by the extent of volunteerism" that is found in a community (Cannuscio, Block, & Kawachi, 2003, p. 395). Participants who are engaged in improving their organizations and businesses through creative action help to build that social capital. In return, those older adults discover that social capital is an "important ingredient for successful aging" (Cannuscio et al., 2003, p. 399). Unfortunately, the authors found that in many communities, social capital is declining. They suggested there is an urgent need for coordinated planning to address this decline, which may only increase as our population continues to age (Cannuscio et al., 2003).

Exploring the Positive Power of the Mature Mind

In his seminal work, *The Creative Age: Awakening Human Potential in the Second Half of Life*, Cohen (2000), former director of the Center on Aging, Health, and Humanities at George Washington University, called for "a new frame of reference in which to picture ourselves growing and (to) recognize how the confluence of inner resources and life circumstances can present us with opportunities to revive our lives in meaningful, satisfying ways" (p. 77). Cohen's career as a physician and psychiatrist focused on older adults and their creative potentials. His research increased our understanding of the mature mind and its capacity for creative expression. In fact, he conjectured, "it may be easier to define problems and come up with strategies" as we get older, as our accumulated "knowledge, our experiences, our emotional history, and our social, career, and life experiences all add to the inner resources that we tap during the creative process" (p. 77). Through a simple formula, conceived in a dream, Cohen (2000) was able to describe the interconnecting factors that influence our creativity:

$$C = me^2$$

The formula proposes that creative expression (C)—a creative accomplishment, product, idea, or understanding—is the product of the mass (m) of knowledge one has accumulated and the external life experiences (e) of daily living—squared: increased exponentially by producing new insights for creativity and self-expression (Cohen, 2000).

Cohen (2005) observed that not only is the healthy, mature brain capable of producing creative ideas, products, and insights, but research studies using PET scans and MRIs revealed four key brain attributes that support a more optimistic view of human potential in the second half of life: 1) scientists now know that the brain re-sculpts itself as a result of new experiences and learning; 2) the brain continues to form new cells; 3) emotional experiences increase the brain's circuitry; and 4) the aging brain utilizes both hemispheres simultaneously, indicating an increase in active functioning (Cohen, 2005, p. 23). Understanding the potential of our elder population should lead to exploring creative ways for our older adults to contribute to their communities. Keeping older community members actively involved with maintaining the vitality of organizations and businesses increases the well-being of all concerned.

The Baby Boomers in Retirement: 70 is the New 50

The generation known as the Baby Boomers, those born between 1946 and 1964, comprise just under 25 percent of the U.S. population (United States Census Bureau, 2015), which suggests they will have a continuing impact on our communities and on our attitudes about aging. Lloyd (2014), a Baby Boomer herself, found that "boomers in general intend to continue having meaningful engagements with their communities and expect to both design and manage activities. They bring myriad skills gained from years of experience" (p. 26). She described herself and her fellow Boomers as:

> having invented the term "over-achiever," redefining the world in our own image, and influencing every trend for more than five decades. We are independent thinkers and delight in never doing what others expect of us. You can call us Boomers, Abbies, or Zoomers, but don't call us senior citizens or old. We are interested in trying new jobs and staying involved. (Lloyd, 2014, p. 26)

When compared to previous generations of retirees, Baby Boomers will have many more productive years after retirement. For instance, Baby Boomers who were 65 and in good health in 2010 can expect to enjoy 10 to 15 more years of productive living (National Center for Health Statistics, 2014).

Cook (2015) wrote that Baby Boomers have been criticized for holding onto "high expectations for their lives and for pushing too hard to meet them. These are qualities, however, that could serve them nicely as they strive to grow older with some comfort and purpose" (para. 2). Cook quoted Coughlin, Director of the Massachusetts Institute of Technology's AgeLab, who said that this generation of retirees "recognize that the current systems in place are not only inadequate to meet the demands of aging, but woefully inadequate to meet their expectations" (para. 2), and that "what we are lacking is not just social services for an aging society but infrastructure for an aging society" (para. 9).

Scharlach, a professor of aging at the University of California (Berkeley) School of Social Welfare who was interviewed by Cook (2015), was confident that the Baby Boomers will offer a model for future generations: "The leading edge of the boomers grew up in the post-World War II years, when everything was possible.... A lot of people don't want to grow old the way their parents did" (para. 11). As this next generation of older adults redefines aging in America, their group mindset, coupled with the latest research on the mature mind and its adaptability, flexibility, and creative potential, challenges our society to invite these experienced elders to design and implement creative solutions to the problems facing them and all of us.

Developing the Well-being of Our Elder Population

Merriam and Kee (2014) articulated the concept of community well-being as being associated with a population that is in good health, socially engaged, and able to handle crises. What contributes to the development of that well-being is tied strongly to the relationship between lifelong learning and an individual's connectedness to his or her community. Merriam and Kee suggested three frameworks that link these elements: aging, lifelong learning, and community well-being. These frameworks or infrastructures of older adult life have been labeled "active aging, productive aging, and positive/successful aging" (p. 132). These are related but distinct concepts. Active aging refers to maintaining physical fitness and an active lifestyle; productive aging includes the ability to create new knowledge and share that knowledge and experience with others; and positive/successful aging includes attention to "psychological and spiritual well-being" (p. 133).

From this framework, it follows naturally that the involvement of seniors in activities such as an applied CPS workshop not only keeps them active and productive, but also allows them the opportunity to bring their valued experiences and knowledge to others, promoting a state of psychological well-being. In essence, engaging older adults in a CPS process to address real challenges in their communities supports active and productive aging and increases the social capital of a community. According to Merriam and Kee (2014), "as older adults become more knowledgeable and more socially engaged, personal as well as community well-being is enhanced" (p. 135).

Senior centers often judge the quality of their programs using the Six Dimensions of Wellness, developed by Hettler (National Wellness Institute, n.d.). Stover, program director for Generations, a senior center in Montgomery County, Pennsylvania, was asked to evaluate two CPS workshops offered at their center ("Introduction to Creative Problem Solving" and the follow-up "Applied CPS," which were mentioned at the start of this paper), in the context of the Six Dimensions. Her response supports the proposition that creative problem solving activities serve the aging population in multiple ways—and in this instance, in five of the six ways measured. Stover wrote:

We survey our participants based on which dimension of wellness we feel that (a) program is focused (on). Some programs may help participants achieve wellness in more than one area.... We felt that [the CPS programs] touched five of the six dimensions. I have highlighted which aspects I feel the particular program you brought to Generations included:

Social: How a person contributes to their environment and their community, and how to build better living spaces and social networks;

Occupational: The enrichment of life through work and its interconnectedness to living and playing;

Spiritual: The development of belief systems, values, and creating a world-view;

Emotional: Self-esteem, self-control, and determination of a sense of direction;

Intellectual: Creative and stimulating mental activities and sharing your gifts with others. (A. R. Stover, personal communication, December 2, 2015)

Creative Problem Solving: A Trusted Process

With the publication of *Applied Imagination: Principles and Procedures of Creative Problem Solving*, Osborn (1953) introduced a process that would deliberately facilitate creative thinking. At first, the idea that creative thinking could be enhanced by techniques that would improve the fluency and flexibility of idea-generation caused some skepticism. However, in subsequent years, with the help of educator Parnes (1992), a model of CPS was introduced to students and organizations, and was studied, verified, and extended. As the model has evolved and extensive research has supported Osborn's premise, CPS has emerged as one of the most effective methods to enhance creativity skills (Puccio & Keller-Mathers, 2007). As communities seek ways to engage their older residents in the challenges of living in the 21st century, and as organizations serving the aging population seek to include the experience and life skills of elders, learning to use the CPS process can be an energizing and collaborative tool to build social capital.

Roles, a program director at Vital Aging Network (VAN) in Minnesota, in an interview with Suttie (2014), expressed concern that "seniors are often seen as people who need services instead of people who have a lot to offer. We focus on community-based development where seniors have the freedom to determine what they need and how to get it" (p. 34). The network trains seniors in community organizing, giving them the skills to assess what their neighborhood needs, gather resources, and start new programs, all steps inherent in a creative problem solving process. Assessing the situation, determining the challenge, generating ideas, choosing the best solutions, finding acceptance, and implementing the plan are all steps in a CPS model that builds collaborative, creative learning (Puccio, Mance, & Murdock, 2011).

Why Teach a Creative Problem Solving Process to Older Adults?

"If not now, when?" is a phrase often uttered by those entering the "liberation stage" of life, a time of experimentation and innovation, when plans are shaped by a sense of personal freedom and more time to do as one chooses. Even new neuron formations accommodate a desire for novelty and inventiveness (Cohen, 2005). Sometime between the late 50s and the mid-70s, individuals experience a sense of freedom. They often find themselves with more choices than they had anticipated. At the same time, many may lose a sense of connectedness to a place of employment and a daily work schedule. Heller and Cheng (2009) found that older citizens can be marginalized, sometimes excluded from social, political, and economic participation, and can suffer from a loss of status when they no longer play key roles in economic production. Now, as citizens of the 21st Century expecting to live active and healthy lives for another decade or two, what skills do they need to help them be of service to their communities, to be part of an interdependent system that provides themselves and others dignity and respect?

The Partnership for 21st Century Learning (n.d.) has created a framework "to define and illustrate the skills and knowledge students need to succeed in work, life and citizenship, as well as the support systems necessary for 21st century learning outcomes" (para. 1). Among the learning and life skills were those embedded in a creative problem solving process: creative (divergent) and critical (convergent) thinking, flexibility, adaptability, collaboration, productivity, and leadership. Also listed were civic literacy, innovation, creativity, and communication. Today's older adults, retiring from careers in business and education, already have strong foundations in many of these skills. Indeed, some retirees used models of CPS in their lives as teachers, scientists, engineers, and architects. For other older adults, learning a CPS process would mean acquiring a new tool, one that could keep them socially connected to new friends and creative thinkers.

Creative Problem Solving Designed for Seniors

The Beckman Institute for Advanced Science and Technology at the University of Illinois is home to Senior Odyssey, a program for creative engagement. Senior Odyssey, a program developed by the Adult Learning Laboratory with support from the National Institute of Aging, was designed to promote cognitive health in older adults through mindful engagement in creative problem solving (Beckman Institute for Advanced Science and Technology, n.d.). Based on the Odyssey of the Mind program for elementary, secondary, and college students, Senior Odyssey involves older adults in a competitive format that includes a long-term, open-ended problem, to engage them "both intellectually and socially by immersing themselves in a variety of mentally-stimulating activities—decision-making, creativity, collaboration, evaluation of ideas, and competition with others" (Adult Learning Lab, n.d.).

Pacific University's Innovative Practice Project created their own senior version of Odyssey of the Mind, which was piloted at the Cornell Estates retirement community (Proctor, Teerlinck, & Willis, 2014). Seniors participating in the program reported satisfaction with the social aspects of working on a team, enjoyment of being able to work with younger adults, and the rewarding nature of creating a final product. Interestingly, while competition is a major part of Odyssey of the Mind at the school level, the competitive aspect of the program seemed not to interest many seniors.

Whether one provides an open-ended challenge to a Senior Odyssey team or whether a client provides a real-life problem facing her organization, the CPS process produces the same types of outcomes for participants. The process draws participants into their community in a way that values their ideas, their teamwork, and their commitment to improving the environment in which they live. Whether competing or not, problem-solving programs clearly support active and productive aging.

Creative Problem Solving Builds Interdependence and Valuable Social Capital

Csikszentmihalyi (1996) stressed the positive impact of what he called "crystallized intelligence" (p. 213). It is what elders bring to the table when they add their creative thoughts to a challenge. Their abilities to make sensible judgments, recognize similarities across different categories, and use deduction and logical reasoning—abilities that depend more on reflection than quick reaction time— have been developed over their six or more decades of learning, work, and life experiences (Csikszentmihalyi, 1996).

Fisher and Specht (1999) examined the relationship between creativity, problem solving, and successful and/or productive aging. They summarized that creativity is related to successful aging since "it fosters a perception of circumstances as opportunities for growth" (p. 469). As with aging, creativity requires an openness to challenges, and a willingness to test one's problem-solving skills to arrive at unique solutions" (p. 469). It seems evident, given the probability of a longer and healthier life, the understanding of the potential of the mature mind, the criteria for well-being, and the need for building the social capital of our communities, that engaging our elders in activities to stimulate their intellectual and creative capacities would truly be a worthwhile investment.

When urban studies theorist Florida (2002) suggested that "strong communities, not institutions within them, are the key to social cohesion" (p. 324), he was describing a society and the rise of a generation of people whose lives relied more on a creative approach to living and working. He stated that the creative class had to address a few fundamental issues, one of which involved our changing demographics. He proposed that we needed to "build new forms of social cohesion in a world defined by increasing diversity and beset by growing fragmentation" (p. 318). He concluded that in order to do this, we must "ensure that the creativity of the many is tapped and that the benefits of the Creative Age are extended to everyone" (p. 318). After all, "the task of building a truly creative society is not a game of solitaire. This game we play as a team" (p. 326).

A Brighter, More Creative Future Awaits

As a practitioner actively engaged in designing and facilitating CPS workshops for older adults, I have seen evidence that CPS builds interdependence and valuable social capital. I saw it in the creative ideas that have become concrete social events and campaigns in our local community. There is proof, too, in the excited questions about forthcoming workshops, and in the smiles, laughter, connectedness, and friendship shared during the creative process.

Much room exists for creative solutions to the challenges of aging productively and successfully in our society. In the new paradigm, perhaps the elders themselves could be the source of those creative solutions. Facilitators of CPS are retiring, as well. Perhaps more of them will discover, as I have, the joy and satisfaction of empowering a population of contemporaries to become change agents in their communities. Communities everywhere will always need to have rich social capital. I can recommend from my experience and from the research presented that there is value in opening the door to a senior center, smelling the coffee, finding new friends, and becoming a facilitative leader who helps build social capital in our aging population.

References

Adult Learning Lab. (n.d.). *Senior odyssey*. Retrieved from http://seniorodyssey.org/about.html

Beckman Institute for Advanced Science and Technology. (n.d.). *Senior odyssey: A program for creative engagement.* Retrieved from http://www.seniorodyssey.org/Senior%20Odyssey%20brochure.pdf

Cannuscio, C., Block, J., & Kawachi, I. (2003). Social capital and successful aging: The role of senior housing. *Annals of Internal Medicine, 139*(5), 395-399.

Cohen, G. D. (2000). *The creative age: Awakening human potential in the second half of life.* New York, NY: Avon Books.

Cohen, G. D. (2005). *The power of the mature mind: The positive power of the aging brain.* New York, NY: Basic Books.

Cook, N. (2015, June 28). *Will baby boomers change the meaning of retirement?* Retrieved from http://www.theatlantic.com/business/archive/2015/06/baby-boomers-retirement/396950/

Csikszentmihalyi, M. (1996). *Creativity: Flow and the psychology of discovery and invention.* New York, NY: HarperCollins.

Fisher, B., & Specht, D. (1999). Successful aging and creativity in later life. *Journal of Aging Studies, 13*(4), 457-472.

Florida, R. L. (2002). *The rise of the creative class: And how it's transforming work, leisure, community and everyday life.* New York, NY: Basic Books.

Heller, K., & Cheng, S. (2009). Global aging: Challenges for community psychology. *American Journal of Community Psychology, 1,* 161-173.

Lloyd, M. (2014). Perspectives of a baby boomer: What boomers will do to and for Oregon libraries. *OLA Quarterly, 13*(1), 26-27.

Merriam, S., & Kee, Y. (2014). Promoting community wellbeing: The case for lifelong learning for older adults. *Adult Education Quarterly, 64*(2), 128-144. doi:10.1177/0741713613513633

National Center for Health Statistics. (2014). United States life tables, 2010. *National Vital Statistics Reports, 63*(7). Retrieved from http://www.cdc.gov/nchs/data/nvsr/nvsr63/nvsr63_07.pdf

National Wellness Institute. (n.d.) *The six dimensions of wellness.* Retrieved from http://www.nationalwellness.org/?page=Six_Dimensions

Osborn, A. F. (1953). Applied imagination: *Principles and procedures of creative problem solving.* New York, NY: Charles Scribner's Sons.

Parnes, S. J. (1992). *Source book for creative problem solving: A fifty year digest of proven innovation processes.* Buffalo, NY: Creative Education Foundation Press.

Partnership for 21st Century Skills. (n.d.). *Framework for 21st century learning.* Retrieved from http://www.p21.org/our-work/p21-framework

Proctor, A., Teerlinck, J., & Willis, B. (2014). *Odyssey of the Mind: Increasing cognitive and social participation in older adults.* Retrieved from http://commons.pacificu.edu/ipp/43/

Puccio, G., & Keller-Mathers, S. (2007). Enhancing thinking and leadership skills through creative problem solving. In A. G. Tan (Ed.), *Creativity: A handbook for teachers* (pp. 281-301). Singapore: World Scientific.

Puccio, G. J., Mance, M., & Murdock, M. C. (2011). *Creative leadership: Skills that drive change* (2nd ed.). Thousand Oaks, CA: Sage Publications.

Suttie, J. (2014, March 14). *How social connections keep seniors healthy.* Retrieved from http://greatergood.berkeley.edu/article/item/how_social_connections_keep_seniors_healthy

United States Census Bureau. (2015). *Millennials outnumber baby boomers and are far more diverse, Census Bureau reports.* Retrieved from http://www.census.gov/newsroom/press-releases/2015/cb15-113.html

About the Author

Virginia (Ginger) Bernd is a founder and executive director of Instar Learning Alliance, an educational non-profit that focuses on building the social capital of our senior population. Her discovery of the Creative Problem Solving Institute (CPSI) in the late 70s had a profound impact on her approach to teaching. Ginger found ways to bring creativity and problem solving into her English classes and designed innovative programs for gifted secondary students. During her professional career, she facilitated strategic planning sessions for school district personnel, applied creative problem solving techniques for community building in Chester, PA, and advocated for the inclusion of creativity and problem solving courses for future teachers. As a teaching colleague of the Creative Education Foundation, Ginger taught the Springboard program, presented extending sessions, and served for several years as the coordinator of CEF's Youthwise program. Now an energetic senior herself, Ginger facilitates workshops for older adults, helping them address community concerns that keep them actively involved in creating positive change.

Email: ggbernd@comcast.net, gingerb@instarlearningalliance.org
Web: instarlearningalliance.org

Acknowledgments

Since she has left the building for a short while, we get the opportunity to recognize the work of Mary Kay Culpepper, co-editor of the last two editions of this series. Mary Kay is a fantastic editor and scholar, and a joy to work with. We wish her well as she pursues a doctorate at the University of Westminster in London.

We also wish to express our gratitude (and occasional awe) for Julia Figliotti, an ICSC alumna and contributor to the 2014 edition, who might just be the best copy editor anywhere.

Our colleagues at the International Center for Studies in Creativity at SUNY Buffalo State deserve special thanks. Gerard Puccio, Creative Studies department chair, and Rita Zientek, associate dean of the School of the Professions, have supported ICSC Press since its inception. Selcuk Acar, John Cabra, Roger Firestien, Jon Michael Fox, Marie Mance, Sue Keller-Mathers, and Jo Yudess continue to nurture and challenge the students who come to the Center, and us, too.

We have spouses who both indulge and encourage us, and so we are especially grateful to Eleanor Reali and Andy Burnett.

Finally, our deepest appreciation goes to the contributors to *Big Questions in Creativity 2016*. They and the many scholars who pass through the ICSC are standard-bearers for creativity, carrying out our mission to ignite creativity around the world, every day, in ways both exquisite and breathtaking.

About the Editors

Paul Reali is the founder of OmniSkills, LLC, a training and facilitation firm in Charlotte, North Carolina, and is the Managing Editor of ICSC Press. Paul has an M.S. in Creativity from the International Center for Studies in Creativity at SUNY Buffalo State, and an M.B.A. from Syracuse University, with a major in innovation management. He is the co-author of *Creativity Rising: Creative Thinking and Creative Problem Solving in the 21st Century,* and the co-editor of *Big Questions in Creativity 2013,* both published by ICSC Press. He is the principal contributor to creativeproblemsolving.com, a resource for CPS practitioners, and has published articles on business and creativity topics in more than a dozen regional, national, and international publications. He is a regular presenter at the annual Creative Problem Solving Institute.

Email: paul@omniskills.com
Twitter: @paulreali
LinkedIn: linkedin.com/in/paulreali
Web: omniskills.com, creativeproblemsolving.com, paulreali.com

Dr. Cyndi Burnett is an Assistant Professor at the International Center for Studies in Creativity at Buffalo State. She has a Bachelor of Fine Arts in Theater, a Master of Science in Creativity, and a Doctorate of Education in Curriculum, Teaching and Learning, all of which she uses to help "ignite creativity around the world." Her research interests include: the use of creative models and techniques with children, creative thinking in higher education, and current trends in creativity. Her work includes projects such as: working with educators to bring creative thinking into the classroom, connecting communities of creative thinkers via social media, and designing and running a Massive Open Online Course (MOOC) on Everyday Creativity.

Dr. Burnett is devoted to creating engaging lessons in education. In addition to teaching creativity professionally, she serves on the Board of Trustees for Elmwood Franklin School in Buffalo, is a Learning Advisor for DIY.org, and is a consulting editor for the *Journal of Creative Behavior.* Dr. Burnett was featured in an article in the *New York Times* titled, "Creativity Becomes an Academic Discipline." She is the co-editor of the *Big Questions in Creativity* book series and co-author of the books *Weaving Creativity into Every Strand of Your Curriculum* and *My Sandwich is a Spaceship: Creative Thinking for Parents and Young Children.*

Twitter: @CyndiBurnett
Facebook: https://www.facebook.com/cyndiaburnett
Email: argonac@buffalostate.edu

About
the International Center for
Studies in Creativity

The International Center for Studies in Creativity (ICSC) is known around the world for its personally transformative undergraduate, graduate and distance programs that cultivate skills in creative thinking, innovative leadership practices and problem solving skills.

ICSC is the first program in the world to teach the science of creativity at a graduate level: Our Graduate Certificate program includes six courses that focus on creative process, facilitation, assessment, training, theory and leadership. With an additional four courses, including a master's project or thesis, students can complete a Master of Science degree in creativity and change leadership. Graduate students can pursue their degree on campus or via the distance program, which offers a blend of on-campus and virtual classrooms.

For nearly 50 years, ICSC is proud to have contributed to seminal research to the field of creativity. ICSC is part of Buffalo State, The State University of New York.

To learn more, please visit creativity.buffalostate.edu.

About ICSC Press

Created in 2012, ICSC Press is the imprint of the International Center for Studies in Creativity. The mission of the press supports the vision of the Center to ignite creativity around the world, facilitating the recognition of creative thinking as an essential life skill. ICSC Press's goal is to put the work of our best teachers, thinkers, and practitioners into the hands of a wide audience, making titles available quickly and in multiple formats, both paper and electronic. Our titles include:

Books

Big Questions in Creativity 2016, Paul D. Reali & Cynthia Burnett, Eds.

Why Study Creativity? Reflections & Lessons from the International Center for Studies in Creativity, Jon Michael Fox & Ronni Lea Fox, Eds.

My Sandwich is a Spaceship, by Cyndi Burnett & Michaelene Dawson-Globus

Big Questions in Creativity 2015, Mary Kay Culpepper & Cynthia Burnett, Eds.

Big Questions in Creativity 2014, Mary Kay Culpepper & Cynthia Burnett, Eds.

Big Questions in Creativity 2013, Cynthia Burnett & Paul D. Reali, Eds.

Creativity Rising: Creative Thinking and Creative Problem Solving in the 21st Century, by Gerard J. Puccio, Marie Mance, Laura Barbero Switalski, & Paul D. Reali

Journals

Business Creativity and the Creative Economy, Mark A. Runco, Ed.

Journal of Genius and Eminence, Mark A. Runco, Ed.

To learn more, to purchase titles, or to submit a proposal, visit icscpress.com.

CPSIA information can be obtained
at www.ICGtesting.com
Printed in the USA
FFOW03n1526020616
24635FF